95

BIM

for Building Owners and Developers

BIM

for Building Owners and Developers

Making a Business Case for Using BIM on Projects

K. Pramod Reddy

WILEY

JOHN WILEY & SONS, INC.

Library of Congress Cataloging-in-Publication Data:

Reddy, K. Pramod.
  BIM for building owners and developers : making a business case for using BIM on projects / K. Pramod Reddy.
     p. cm.
  Includes bibliographical references and index.
    ISBN 978-0-470-90598-2 (acid-free paper); 978-1-118-12886-2 (e-bk); 978-1-118-12887-9 (e-bk); 978-1-118-12977-7 (e-bk); 978-1-118-12978-4 (e-bk); 978-1-118-12979-1 (e-bk)

1. Building information modeling.   2. Real estate developers.   I. Title.   II. Title: Building information modeling for building owners and developers.
  TH438.13.R44 2011
  333.33'80683–dc23

                                                                        2011040420

Printed in the United States of America

  10 9 8 7 6 5 4 3 2 1

Contents

Preface

Over the last 30 years, industries such as manufacturing, distribution, and finance have been automated, driving enormous gains in productivity worldwide. The exception is the architecture, engineering, and construction industry (AEC). That is, until recently. Maybe this was a function of an ingrained approach industry-wide toward delivering services on an unbundled basis, or maybe the industry was simply slow to embrace the benefits of integrated data management. However, over the last 5 years, with the ramping up of building information modeling (BIM) and new, subsequent developments and applications, the AEC world moved firmly into the middle of a true sea change.

The winners most certainly will be firms that have embraced this new approach toward gathering, processing, and utilizing information across the spectrum of consulting, design, implementation, and operations. Moreover, these new technologies are driving the further growth of integrated EPC and DB services, as the real power lies with access to, development and manipulation of, and pull-through application of data from the start of a capital expense project all the way to monitoring ongoing operations.

While the AEC world is ramping up its intelligence around the use of BIM and a multitude of related new applications, the next evolution of application lies with building owners. In addition, this new intelligence of leveraging data to analyze and model results is used to drive efficiencies, and builder/owners are witnessing a change in applications that are available to drive building and system life cycle efficiencies.

BIM for Building Owners and Developers takes the reader through the multitude of opportunities and challenges in quickly moving "up the BIM curve" while overviewing both strategic frameworks and technical information along the way, with features such as "A Tales from the Trenches" that highlight real-life applications.

The world of BIM is rapidly developing, with new applications emerging almost daily, including serious work around artificial intelligence (AI), driving significant next-generation opportunities. Building owners who are well educated on the topic and embrace these new technologies will have a clear advantage in their industry going forward.

Grant G. McCullagh
Former Vice Chairman AECOM
and CEO, President GIBS LLC

(Mr. McCullagh is a 30-year veteran of the AEC industry, having served additionally as Chairman of the Design/Build Institute of America, Chairman/CEO/CoFounder of McClier, and Chairman or CEO of numerous other worldwide AEC firms.)

Acknowledgments

Thanks to my wife Nehal and my boys, Devan and Jaimin. My wife has always been supportive of my career. She had to endure not only my hectic travel schedule but also my disappearances to "work on the book" after having been gone all week. Thanks also to my boys, who struggled to understand why daddy was always so tired.

This book is dedicated to my father, K. Pulla Reddy, who influenced me in becoming part of the architecture, engineering, and construction industry at a very young age.

chapter

1

Introduction to Building Information Modeling

Building information modeling is most often referred to as BIM. In practice, BIM is defined as the file that is created by the use of three-dimensional (3-D) computer-aided design (CAD) software programs. Unfortunately, this is the broadest definition and is often the root cause of failure in the deployment of BIM. The focus on BIM as being an "upgrade" to the latest CAD software is the first step many firms take in the wrong direction. In reality, BIM is a process improvement methodology that leverages data to analyze and predict outcomes throughout different phases of the building life cycle.

While there are several books in the marketplace addressing the technical aspects of BIM, including software training manuals, the focus of this book has been to look at BIM from a building owner's perspective. To date, the owner's role in BIM has primarily been as the recipient of the "BIM" at the end of the project. The reality is that the owner is the most pertinent participant in the BIM process. This book is not intended to be a technology-driven perspective of BIM but rather a tool for an owner to better understand BIM in order to deploy practical initiatives that lead to BIM being beneficial for the owner's projects.

BIM is a "paradigm shift"—and, in most cases, a paradigm shift happens quickly. For various reasons, however, the architecture, engineering, and construction (AEC) community is moving through this shift at a much slower pace. The major reason for this lethargic adaptation is due to the nature of the construction system at large. It exists as a highly fragmented environment, supporting an ecosystem consisting largely of influencers that consist of highly repetitive experience with a single decision maker— the owner—with relatively nominal experience compared to the ecosystem. The current state of the AEC processes and the end state of the paradigm shift are both well understood. The adaptation from the current to the end state is creating the most chaos. It is important to understand that the notion of BIM as a process improvement technology is more conceptual than analytical. To deem an improvement of process implies the measurement of existing systems and documentation of these metrics as a baseline for improvement.

BIM instills a vision of what the future of construction can become in terms of "hard" improvements. BIM is also an essential platform today to measure and collect data for existing process metrics. The single mission of this book is to engage with the *most* experienced stakeholders in the AEC industry. Software is just a tool and, like many tools, is misused by practitioners with the *least* amount of experience.

The information age has created a platform for transparency in almost every industry, except the construction industry. The challenge has been the ability for the "consumer" (in this case the owner) to drive and demand change.

This book covers both basic and more complex BIM topics. It also incorporates a blend of management consulting and technology principles. It is meant to be used either in parts or in its entirety, based on the needs of the owner. This book contains a lot of content and concepts that are meant to drive awareness for discussion and not necessarily for practical implementation. The majority of the book is derived from years of practical experience in the field. Many practical examples are presented in this book in a special feature called "A Tale from the Trenches."

The purpose of these tales from the trenches is to demonstrate specific workflows along with the challenges and benefits of using BIM. These were developed from actual projects but modified and made anonymous so that there is a clear and honest insight. One of the single most important challenges within the AEC community is honestly regarding the actual utilization of BIM and the challenges associated with BIM implementation.

In many chapters, there are quotes from other books that are relevant to the subject matter. These should also be considered recommended reading for your organization.

The purpose of this book is to provide a framework for building owners and developers to drive BIM objectives that substantiate their objectives and guide their AEC vendor community to compliance. Much of the information about the methods of the AEC community at large provides a baseline for how BIM is being used currently and are not necessarily best practices. Owners can demand a better process with greater transparency if they truly understand the opportunities and limitations of the technology, the industry, and the future. This book can be read from beginning to end but is also designed to be used as a reference for owners that are facing a particular challenge.

Technology should drive benefit to the consumer. Prior to the Internet age, a consumer went to a travel agent to book travel, hotels, and rental cars. There was no transparency of flight schedules, rates, availability, and quality. The travel agent acted as a proxy of the consumer to fulfill his or her needs but was compensated by the travel industry. Consumers were required to "trust" their travel agents. The rule of thumb "to trust but verify" was difficult because there was no method of verification. Technology made it possible to shrink the sales channel and disintermediate the supply chain. Consumers were given the ability to both trust and verify the pricing and availability from their travel agents.

The AEC community and the construction industry at large are built with layers of agents that may or may not create value for the owner. In many cases, as in the case of many general contractors, the value may only be the subordinated risk of contracting with a single party. This is of value to many owners, but the value may not be justified by the price. In lieu of purely subordinating risk, an owner should be able to mitigate risk by leveraging data. This type of data is generally referred to as decision support data and is common in most other industries.

The History of BIM

One of the most vivid statements I remember from my father was that the most intelligent people in the room are the ones who are silent. I have really used this in understanding "why BIM matters." I have found that the discussions around BIM tend to be driven vocally by those in an organization who "know it all" but have never actually built a building. The experienced people tend to remain silent—or, better yet, bored. The most experienced professionals in our industry understand that the success of any technology is driven by the weakest link in the ecosystem. For a better understanding of this, refer to the history of BIM. This, to the dismay of many of my peers, is to ignore the technology aspects of BIM in its entirety because BIM is a paradigm shift, and it is much more than technology. Instead, I have focused on spending my time with the most experienced individuals in the construction industry. This time is spent trying to understand reality versus fiction.

The start of design documentation was the creation of a new language to communicate the three-dimensional (3-D) world (reality) in a two-dimensional (2-D) communication platform. This platform was the first in creating a language in 2-D that could be universally understood. This 2-D platform consisted of plan and elevation views with a level of development (LOD) that was communicated with details, sections, and specifications.

It was also clear that in this 2-D platform there would be gaps in information that would be subject to interpretation. Because, realistically, how could the real world be communicated in a 2-D document? The phrase "do not see the movie, read the book instead" has been heard many times by most individuals. The book leaves so much for our own individual interpretation (and imagination) that reading becomes a highly individualized experience. Conversely, the movie is very specific, and we tend to stretch to develop our individual interpretations of the movie from our own experience. This may work in the entertainment world, but in the world of construction, interpretation leads to so much variability that expectations are hardly in-line with each stakeholder. This interpretation is obviously biased—not only by each stakeholder's role but also by budgetary concerns.

BIM software by definition is a subset of CAD software, but BIM processes are very different from CAD processes. The traditional process of developing construction drawings began by using mechanical methods (pen/paper, ink/vellum, etc.). With the advent of CAD, this mechanical process was moved to the computer screen, where it was transformed into a computing process. The deliverables remained unchanged, but the speed and precision those computers were able to bring to the development of construction drawings was accelerated. Additionally, the rate of incorporating design changes was vastly affected. Therefore, the design process was not affected by this technology as much as the production process. This is directly analogous to the change from a typewriter to a word processor program on a computer. CAD provided some design-assist tools that allowed for precise dimensioning, easy editing, and cut-and-paste functions. CAD has historically been used as a design authoring tool.

As a result of the increase in computing power and the decrease in price, many in our industry have come to use CAD to collaborate during the design process. With the advent of easy-to-use Internet-based file-sharing technologies, the AEC industry has become fairly efficient during the design phase. These CAD programs have also been capable of producing 3-D CAD models for the purposes of visualization. Additional applications were developed to extend basic CAD functionality to link this information to databases and automated routines (scripting macros). Traditional CAD, however, has played a very minor role in optimizing the overall construction process. To say that BIM is "just another CAD program" would be the equivalent of saying that computer spreadsheets are "just another calculator."

The current standard of construction documentation is interpreted to build the "reality" 3-D model (i.e., the building), while BIM is used to create a "virtual" 3-D model to build construction documentation (CDs). These CDs are then interpreted and used in a traditional construction process. In essence, today's construction environment sees BIM being used as a CAD application. This process is changing quite rapidly and being mostly driven by owners and contractors. CAD is used to develop information that is used in the life cycle of the building which is then aggregated into the building. BIM is used to develop an aggregation of building information that is then extracted throughout the life cycle of the building.

In summary, BIM is a database-driven representation of the building throughout the building's life cycle. While 3-D is an important part of BIM, it is only a small part of its capability.

The construction industry moves at a very deliberate pace. While this pace may not seem aggressive, it is indeed progressing. The goal of this book is to provide a guideline for owners to create a plan that is evolutionary and iterative in nature. It is easy to know where owners are (as-is condition) in comparison to where they need to be (to-be condition) in a paradigm shift. The challenge is all of the steps in between. These are analyzed through a process called gap analysis, and I will explore these concepts—as well as how to apply these tools—in later chapters.

BIM can be broken down into different but similar database sets that are based on the author and use of the information:

- Design intent model (by the designer for the designer)
- Build intent model (by the contractor for the contractor)
- Fabrication intent model (by the subcontractor for the subcontractor)
- Facility management model (by the owner for the owner)

Most new systems are first misunderstood and then misused, which consequently results in poor outcomes that are soon after dismissed. Due to the similarity of information, there is a belief that information created by the designer for the designer will somehow be useful for the contractor. The management of building data is a role that is commonly used on large projects. With the advent of BIM, it is becoming a necessity on projects of any size. The amount of data created by BIM is (at a minimum) tenfold that of typical projects using 2-D plans and specifications only. Simply managing data is now becoming a full-time job.

BIM is a transformative technology, very similar to the Internet. Much like Internet adoption, it is initially being used to automate known workflows and legacy information. As this technology becomes better understood, it will soon be used to change and improve construction processes. Fundamentally, the owner community has not benefited from the information age, while the advent of technology has created a high level of transparency to the consumer. BIM is changing the owners' processes and shaping the way they do business.

Future Trends

Discussing future trends prior to current trends may seem counterintuitive, but the future opportunities of BIM will spur the current investment required to take advantage of these future trends. Current BIM adoption and use is on a project basis for managing and driving successful project outcomes. The most interesting aspect of BIM in the long term is the application of data mining and analysis. Once the aggregation of sufficient structured data about buildings throughout their life cycle has taken place, there will be amazing applications. This data can be organized and used as benchmarking and knowledge base data. For instance, the ability to "load" a BIM model and a construction schedule, analyze potential construction delays based on a building system, and determine the average durations of past projects will ultimately help optimize design.

Predictive Maintenance

The use of BIM data to drive predictive maintenance on a building is still in its early stages but is, in fact, growing. Analyzing the BIM data across a portfolio of buildings while being able to determine maintenance cycles on major and minor building systems allows for fewer unplanned outages as well as greater precision in operational budgeting. Additionally, being able to benchmark against similar buildings (and portfolios of buildings) will assist in assessing comparative performance.

Constructability Analysis

Constructability analysis is an area that is also growing rapidly. The concept of simulating the construction process and predicting outcomes has a tremendous benefit to owners. It has become the next generation of a traditional plan review service. While a plan review service can create value, because it functions as a peer review, it is indeed quite limiting. A BIM-based constructability analysis provides the base benefit of a traditional plan review in addition to the by-products of BIM-based simulation. The ability to aggregate constructability data and analyze it against actual outcomes allows owners to understand the quality of the work product from their design teams and, more specifically, how it drives construction delays and budget overruns. An example of BIM analytics and the extension of these analytics to the owner's benefit is the iBIM Constructability Index (CI). Our team at ARC developed this tool to assist owners in scoring the constructability of a building project.

The iBIM CI is a proprietary benchmarking system. The system is used to provide a project-specific risk rating that can be used to mitigate construction risk. Based on the quantity and severity of the discrepancies, the CI can rate each discipline performance and then combine the scores for a total project score. On a scale of 0 to 100 percent, 0 represents the worst outcomes and 100 percent represents the best outcomes. Listed below is each discipline with its corresponding CI score and an overall project score.

These efforts result in significant payback to the proposed project; this process has provided cost reductions of between 5 and 20 percent, benefit/cost ratios of up to 10:1, and large schedule reductions. The intangible benefits are as important as the quantitative benefits and must be recognized accordingly. These include more accurate contract documents by reducing requests for information (RFIs) and change orders, reduced schedule impact, increased productivity, and improvement in the sequence of construction.

Product Manufacturer Analysis

A typical building consists mostly of manufactured products. The building product manufacturers (BPMs) are vital members of the construction ecosystem. Although they have already become involved with the BIM process, it is still early for many of these BPMs. Some of these provide product information models (PIMs) for use in BIM software, which centers on the concept that, as virtual buildings are created, virtual products will need to be installed in the virtual buildings. These PIMs need to resemble the actual product as closely as possible. Like the rest of the industry, BPMs have suffered a few "false starts" in providing this information. These challenges are caused by the BPMs' mind-set of treating this information like CAD details, without truly understanding the BIM process. BIM drives a need to understand the construction *process* and the product, not just the construction *content* and the product. There have been encouraging signs from some BPMs that are making significant commitments to be part of the ecosystem rather than existing as mere suppliers to the ecosystem.

The BPM community is now adapting many of its configuration tools to work within BIM software or be compatible with BIM file formats. Many BPM companies have added BIM capability to their support staff so that they can truly collaborate on projects. Connectivity to product availability and pricing configuration is not currently a focus but will be the next step in BIM adoption. (See Figure 1.1.)

Building Management Systems

Integration of building management systems (also called building automation systems) and BIM is a growing trend. The concept of

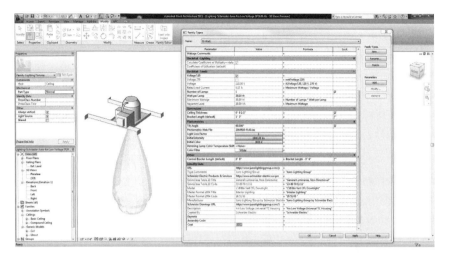

Figure 1.1 Installed information of a system.

intelligent buildings has been around for several decades. The challenge has generally been the ability to have detailed information about the building, its systems and intelligence. Now that many new buildings will have detailed building information from the BIM, integrating this data into intelligent building management systems becomes seamless. These systems are a combination of software and hardware. The software is used to create a command and control environment to manage almost all aspects of a building. The hardware consists of supporting systems for the software but more uniquely the digital control systems that control building systems. Much like a standard office computer network is a series of connected systems, a building management system is a network of connected building systems. These building systems include occupancy; security; heating, ventilating, and air conditioning (HVAC); lighting; hot/cold water systems; fire protection and alarms; window shades; room automation (video projectors, drop-down screens, etc.); and communication systems. These systems can be very complex and often include a series of vendors for each specialized system. The ability to use BIM to design and systematically implement and integrate these systems is critical. The other benefit of building management systems is that the building begins to behave much like a typical computer system. This gives an owner the ability to review the log history and generate analytics regarding building performance. This data can be used for future building modifications as well as knowledge for any new facilities that are being designed. These systems can also execute standard routines for a building. These routines would automate a set of events based on a use case. For example, a morning start-up routine for a building would be a combination of security events, HVAC events, and alarm systems. The system would unlock the external doors and restricted corridors, turn on the air conditioning, and switch alarms to passive mode in restricted areas. While this would be a typical recurring event, unplanned events can be developed for automated routines. These could include anything from a water leak to a terrorist threat.

Building management systems are becoming highly sophisticated neurosystems for the building. The costs associated with operating a building combined with the green initiatives that many companies are driving make building management systems a must. The technology is becoming more widely available and with better capability for integration. Many building owners may have a system for their core buildings and are now having to integrate into the tenant-specific system. More important, these systems are now more interconnected with the user community of a building. Consider the following example. A user swipes his or her access card to enter a building after hours. Upon swiping the card, the building knows that the user is an executive who occupies a certain office in the building. The lighting system turns on lights for this executive only in the path to his or her office. The office and adjacent break room lighting and climate controls are engaged. The executive completes his or her work. Upon exiting the building, the executive swipes his or her card, and the building knows to turn off the respective systems. This use case is readily available today and is being used. This innovation and integration has attracted many information technology (IT) systems companies to this space, including Cisco and IBM. It has also begun to blur the responsibilities of the facility manager and IT manager. Buildings are starting to behave much more like an IT system than a building system.

Facility Management Systems

Facility management (FM) systems are adopting the ability to integrate into BIM technology as well. This will allow an owner to click on a system in the BIM and understand such items as install date, who installed it, maintenance performed, and warranty information. This provides an owner with rich information about its building assets. Additionally, an owner is able to communicate with maintenance companies, contractors, and so on with more information during discovery, without having to pay for a subcontractor to determine existing conditions. This will ultimately drive more competitive behavior while at the same time lowering costs.

To discuss how BIM pertains to facility management, let's first discuss typical FM core processes and how they can benefit from the use of technology. These core processes are facility maintenance, asset management, space management, move management, and strategic planning.

Facility Maintenance

Facility maintenance refers to the upkeep, support, and maintenance of building equipment. Facility managers typically keep an inventory and detailed history of equipment and related maintenance requirements, enabling their organizations to extend the life of valuable equipment. Facility managers need to coordinate supervisors, technicians, workshops, and outside vendors to complete facility maintenance tasks. They must also record contract expirations in a database in order to reference or define automated alerts required for preventive maintenance.

From a process perspective, facility managers should incorporate automation for the tracking and reporting of critical data associated with service requests, such as repair costs, response time, and work history. Efficient facility managers use self-service request forms and work order status views for internal customers, send e-mail reminders to themselves and to their vendors for preventive maintenance tasks, and create maintenance tickets automatically for scheduled maintenance jobs. Additionally, the facility manager will route work orders to internal staff and vendors and run reports on various vendors and equipment to analyze costs.

Asset Management

Asset management describes the process of tracking multiple classes of assets—office equipment, furniture, computers, life safety systems, building systems, lab equipment, corporate artwork, and so on.

Assets can be linked within a BIM model to show location, owner-ship, and access to product information—which can greatly improve efficiencies in maintenance and personnel move processes. An effec-tive facility manager will track and locate in a BIM model or on floor plans such corporate assets and define processes for tracking such things as costs, disposition, availability, and assignment.

Space Management

Designed to give facility professionals, departmental liaisons, and executive management complete visibility into workspace occupancy, space management describes the process of managing real-time infor-mation related to the use of space in an organization. A facility man-ager needs to plan, track, and report employee moves, in addition to tracking the notification process. Space management processes allow the facility manager to effectively plan and manage new employee installations as well as move team members and outsourced vendors to new facility locations.

Move Management

This aspect describes the processes that allow the facility manager to plan, track, and report employee moves. Facility managers need to be able to effortlessly coordinate move liaisons as well as move team mem-bers and outsourced vendors. For example, move management can be used to automate existing employees who need to submit move requests to a manager, who will then notify the facility manager for coordination, approval, scheduling, and completion of workspace installation.

Strategic Planning

Strategic planning allows for multiple "what-if" scenarios and visual depictions of an organization's current and future space and occu-pancy rate, using forecasting tools to align a company's space portfo-lio with its business requirements.

Facility managers will need to maintain an accurate inventory of space, such as locations, room numbers, space types, areas, and capacities. The goal of the strategic planning process is to give facility professionals, departmental liaisons, and executive management complete visibility into space and occupancy. The facility manager should seek to centralize space and occupancy information across all locations, provide visibility to management and internal customers, and empower departmental liaisons to manage and maintain space and occupancy information. The facility manager will also improve occupancy rates and space utilization with detailed space inventories, accurate occupancy data, and facility benchmarks.

Software Tools

Many vendors provide software tools that use a core component along with additional modular applications, each focused on the different aspects or processes associated with facility management. These systems should act as a central FM database, which can be accessed and utilized throughout a building's life cycle.

Typically, these programs work as integrated packages of powerful Web-based workplace management products that allow an organization to share information and manage processes that impact the entire facility. Such FM software tools ideally can be accessed by all employees using standard Web browsers, and they feature intuitive interfaces to provide access to key facility information such as floor plans, reports, employee information, and critical documents. These software packages are typically referred to as computer-aided facility management (CAFM) and computerized maintenance management system (CMMS).

CAFM software automates many of the typical functions of facility management. The International Facility Management Association (IFMA) classifies facility management responsibilities into several major functional areas:

- Long-range and annual facility planning
- Facility financial forecasting
- Real estate acquisition and/or disposal
- Work specifications, installation, and space management
- Architectural and engineering planning and design
- New construction and/or renovation
- Maintenance and operations management
- Telecommunications integration, security, and general administrative services

Asset Management Software

Effective asset management software will use graphical queries to search for and visually display assets on floor plans. The system will allow the facility manager to define the method by which to track asset depreciation for financial reporting and compliance, as well as ownership and product information such as serial numbers and installation dates. Asset management systems can also be integrated with other systems, such as bar codes or enterprise resource planning (ERP) systems, making asset tracking efforts more robust.

Space Management Software

Facility managers must be empowered to plan visitor installations on digital floor plans or BIM models. Visitors need to be able to submit their requests to the facility manager via electronic forms, which are then automatically routed through the approval process. Additionally, the AutoCAD integration component of many space management software systems enables users to link a Revit model and AutoCAD drawings to their FM databases. Through menu selection, this link allows for a bidirectional update of key information such as room IDs, personal room assignments, departments, area measurements, and other corresponding information that the organization may require.

The platform also needs to be able to coordinate move details efficiently for people, assets, and infrastructure components. An effective software solution will manage space requests, so that they can be forwarded to the facility manager for coordination, approval, scheduling, and completion. The platform should also allow employees to have the ability to report on every stage of the process.

Move Management Software

Move management software can enable internal customers to submit their own move requests via Web-based forms, which are automatically routed through the approval process. The move requests can be forwarded to the facility manager for coordination, approval, scheduling, and completion, and employees have the ability to report on every stage of the process. Effective software platforms contain the ability to coordinate move details quickly for people, assets, and infrastructure components.

Strategic Planning Software

The facility manager will typically gather and forecast space needs by growth criteria, such as head count, staff detail, area, and percentage growth, before utilizing a platform to assign an employee to a new space. A facility manager will also use a system that considers adjacency, stacking, and other factors that will determine the new employee's location. The platform will need to be able to run reports on space and occupancy projections as well as be able to automate notification to workspace vendors and laborers.

Additionally, the modern facility manager will need to link facility information to detailed spatial information in Revit and use a Web browser to navigate and visualize real-time facility data on the floor plans. This platform should also allow the user to compare utilization data with portfolio performance as well as link space to groups and cost centers to track use of space by department and support space chargeback policies.

Many strategic space planning platforms will also contain an integration component that enables an organization's users to link a Revit model and AutoCAD drawings to the building databases. This link should allow for a bidirectional update of key information such as room IDs, personal room assignments, departments, area measurements, and other corresponding information that the organization requires.

CMMS is sometimes referred to as enterprise asset management because it is focused on managing facilities as an asset, including maintenance. Maintaining an asset ensures the long-term value of the asset, but tracking all activities associated with the asset provides not only proof but also data for future maintenance costs. Many owners retain more detailed information about their fleet of vehicles than their $20 million building asset. This is a challenge because of the vast amount of data to be tracked in a building. BIM and CMMS systems assist owners in overcoming this challenge.

Facility Maintenance Software

Facility maintenance software should enable the facility manager to keep an inventory and detailed history of building equipment and related maintenance requirements. Many platforms allow the team to receive e-mail reminders for routine tasks (such as six-month checkups on air-conditioning units and copiers) and automatically create a maintenance ticket in the system. Generally, facility maintenance platforms will allow the facility manager to maintain an inventory of building equipment with maintenance and cost history as well as automate preventive maintenance scheduling and work orders. FM platforms also associate critical data with self-service requests, such as repair costs, response time, and work history to be tracked, reported, and monitored.

In summary, using FM software tools allows the facility manager to effectively plan new and existing employee moves, manage visitor installations, reconfigure rooms and workspaces, track assets, and manage the entire facility. The facility manager should also seek to improve internal customer service, so the software used should allow the manager to access property information with a map-based interface, run live reports, view floor plans, search archived drawings and critical documents, and share facility data with management, partners, and internal customers within a corporate intranet. The combination of software accessibility via a Web browser interface with the intuitive interface of BIM will provide data to the entire owner enterprise and not just a few that manage the software. This will not only create value to the owner/user community but also will decentralize the collection of data. The decentralization of data creates an environment where data is kept more current and where it becomes more useful and reliable to the user community.

> Organizations would never try to build a new building without detailed and correct drawings, yet they rebuild facilities piece by piece every three to six years without correct drawings because they have never provided for staff to update the original drawings properly. Once BIM becomes standard, the problem will be lessened to the degree that we are willing to constantly keep our drawings updated. For those of us who have a large inventory of older buildings with building drawings of uncertain validity, it is worthwhile to systematically have those buildings surveyed, their systems categorized and their drawings brought up-to-date. BIM should be the standard for all new construction and for major renovations. The ability to conduct BIM and to receive the data may well determine which consultants we use and which building automation system we move forward with.[1]

Building Owner Objectives

BIM is a digital database of physical and functional characteristics that also contains information about a building that can be viewed in more than three dimensions. It enables an organization to virtually build the building as it would be constructed on-site before the actual construction has started. This helps to eliminate many of the inefficiencies of the construction process. The information updated in the BIM at each phase by the team members can be transferred to the next phase without any loss or duplication of information. The model can be accessed by any stakeholder for entering, updating, or extracting information at any point during construction. Upon completion, the data-rich model can be delivered to the owner or the facility manager. This model can then be used for operating the building throughout its entire life cycle. In summary, this is the vision of BIM—but currently there are many factors that do not make this feasible.

BIM has proven to have benefits for every key player in the construction process—from design to construction to facility management. A building owner holds special incentives to implement BIM, not just for the construction of the building but for the maintenance as well. Owners like the General Services Administration (GSA) and the U.S. Army Corps of Engineers (USACE) have taken extreme steps regarding mandating the use of BIM. They believe that BIM adoption should not be driven by cost savings alone but for its other benefits such as the ability to explore different engineering systems, perform energy analysis for Leadership in Energy and Environmental Design (LEED) certification, generate specifications automatically, and eventually eliminate the use of paper and paper-based processes. BIM can be used for creating as-built documentation for existing buildings, space reporting, and spatial and tenant management as well as for evaluating how well a proposed design meets the program requirements. BIM-enabled project owners gain a much higher confidence level about the design and overall construction of their buildings. BIM reduces overall project delivery time in the design phase while reducing the contractor's uncertainty. Consequently, this leads to a more accurate cost picture with more consistent bids.

BIM has dramatically changed the construction process. Construction has been known for its notorious relations involving the contracts among team members. According to the Construction

Users Roundtable (CURT) publication WP1202, 30 percent of the cost of construction is wasted in the field due to coordination errors, wasted material, labor inefficiencies, and other problems that arise during the traditional course of construction. Even though owners may know many of the facts and "numbers," they still accept the price of waste as a part of the overall construction cost. They then build this cost into their estimate, budget, fee, and contingency— which is all ultimately paid by the owner. One of the major causes of these inefficiencies is the horizontal and fragmented supply chain arrangement in the AEC industry, where information is passed from one party to the next in a linear fashion. Each party has its own vested misaligned interest and goals toward the project. In order for owners to realize their own objectives, they should modify this arrangement by engaging the entire team to work "outside of the norm" and under one umbrella, adopting new, more efficient methods of project delivery.

In order to improve efficiency in project delivery, the entire process must achieve a higher level of coordination. This can be achieved through better integration of information and improving process optimization. BIM is a tool that promotes much more detailed collaboration from early on in the life of the project. Many owners require an integrated project delivery (IPD) approach in their projects, which is a reinitialized method of project partnering that uses the talent, experience, and input of all the team members starting at the beginning of the project. However, owners implementing IPD must think outside of the box to leverage BIM for its maximum capability. In an IPD arrangement, all of the project members have one common goal—the success of the project. In theory, this method increases the value for the owner by reducing waste and optimizing efficiency. The IPD process is usually applied throughout the life cycle of the project, which starts with design and fabrication and then continues through the completion of construction. By following this process, an owner reaps the benefits of engaging the construction team early in the design stage for their vital contribution on constructability analysis and value engineering. Owners should also realize that, in an IPD arrangement, the benefit is to the entire team, and there is both mutual risk and reward. In many ways, IPD is a more creative way of subordinating a portion of the risk while also benefiting from a part of the reward. BIM creates a platform that makes it possible to bring in all of the team members at an early stage so as to further increase each other's value and effectiveness. A contractor can start working on constructability analysis of the design even when the design is in an early and incomplete state.

BIM also creates an effective lean process for construction. Lean refers to a process or philosophy of reducing waste (time, material, and labor) and increasing value. The lean process has been applied to manufacturing and is now making its way into construction. The fundamental focus of lean is the concept that *anything* that does not create value to the consumer is considered waste. Value is not a subjective attribute but rather a financially motivated metric. Owners must understand their value drivers before undertaking any type of construction project. Fundamentally, value drivers are different for each owner. Typically, the waste embedded in the process includes change orders, poor information flow, rework, and so on. BIM, when coupled with lean, creates a tool for reducing waste and improving the overall process of project delivery. It achieves significant improvement by simulating the building process in a virtual environment and provides a better analysis with significant documentation. Utilizing BIM along with lean reduces the overall cost of the project by identifying issues at a time when they are still inexpensive to fix or at a time when the value to the owner can be determined. BIM also provides owners with vital decision support data, so that they can better understand the true value of a design change prior to construction. The cost of any change in the construction is inversely proportional to the point in time at which it occurs. In current practice, it is not uncommon to find most of the changes on-site during construction at a point at which the cost of making these changes is not manageable or possibly even feasible for the owner.

There is a general misconception in the construction industry that IPD is required for BIM to be effective. Another is that the owner and the AEC community are working as a team. In the majority of IPD projects (or attempts), the alignments of cost, benefit, and risk have not been shared. In some ways, the classic situation of "quality, schedule, and cost: pick any two" is prevalent. Upon completion of an IPD project, most owners will agree that IPD allowed them to execute the project, beat the schedule, and ultimately deliver a quality product. However, price was sacrificed in the process. Technology should allow us to improve quality, schedule, *and* cost at the same time. Typically, the only sacrifice that is made is in the area of human interaction. With this in mind, it is essentially the owner and their vendors (the AEC community) who focus on delivering on price, quality, and schedule by leveraging technology.

> It has gone so far that many teams in today's companies are not true teams at all; they are not simply set up to work together effectively organizationally, structurally, or motivationally. Branding "Teams" to a project is simply placing vague labels placed on random groupings, or even the entire organization as a whole. These labels accomplish nothing. Frankly, someone has told leadership that they should have teams, and so they have them. Make no mistake, employees are not fooled. They continue to operate as groups or departments of people that simply have the blanket of "team" thrown upon them. Look further and you'll find a group of individuals largely fending for themselves.[2]

User Experience

"User experience" is a term that has historically been reserved for the software design community. While most believe that user experience is explicit to how a user feels when using software, this is a subjective view. In fact, user experience is scientific, and in most cases, the user community is fairly predictable. When the World Wide Web was in early adoption, Web sites were designed in many different ways. Over time, the layout of a Web site came to be quite predictive. When users on the Web are surveyed to provide site usability, the outcomes are typically the same. This recurring comfort that is developed then becomes the standard. In many ways, the user experience for an owner has not changed much over the years. The deliverables are the same, and the interactions with both the design and build community have been consistent. Technology has only shaped the efficiency and automation of manual efforts but has not made a noticeable change to the core process.

The term is applicable to BIM from many different aspects. BIM should be driving a new user experience for the owner. The owner, in turn, should be changing the user experience for its user community. Unfortunately, design review meetings have continued to be the same. The designer meets with the owner to review plans, renderings, and the like and to receive feedback. With the advent of BIM, the designer may arrive with a 3-D model, spin it around a bit, and, after an uproar of applause, move through the meeting. In this case, BIM has been leveraged for the visualization aspect only, but the process has remained the same. Buildings are highly complex, and BIM has helped in creating an environment by which an individual's inability to read construction drawings has not limited his or her ability to provide input to the design process. An owner representative's job is to drive the process to the benefit of all of the stakeholders. This includes the building users, maintenance workers, and so on. Between the advent of distributed computing and BIM, the ability to involve the stakeholders in the design process is an exciting opportunity. This can be accomplished by a method known as crowdsourcing.

Crowdsourcing is the process by which tasks normally performed by employees are outsourced to large groups of users or consumers. Crowdsourcing has become a standard procedure for Web application deployment. Common are beta programs that many companies like Google deploy, where users can utilize the technology in return for providing feedback. Private crowdsourcing is being used to solve complex problems in health sciences by posting a product development challenge to a group and offering a fee to the person who solves the

Figure 1.2 Talent in the cloud. *Courtesy Buffi Aguero*

problem. In some cases, these fees are in the hundreds of thousands of dollars. The leverage of knowledge from many users provides the benefit of mass knowledge as well as specialized knowledge.

For example, a hospital has many constituents in a new building program. In the past, an owner community would be formed to provide and represent the needs of the constituent stakeholders. Using BIM and other collaborative technologies, a hospital would set up a Web portal that included the BIM model. When executing the utilization viewer technologies, a link would be sent to the user community. These users, such as doctors, nurses, financial analysts, medical equipment suppliers, patients, and maintenance workers, would view and walk through the BIM in order to provide structured feedback. This feedback might not exclusively pertain to space use and needs but might even include the use of specific products and equipment. It would create an overall user experience for all of the hospital stakeholders. For instance, if the maintenance team could see the flooring products that are being used, they could provide feedback that the product being considered is high maintenance and would require outside contracting maintenance. Other examples would include a product manufacturer suggesting that there is a newer product that is more efficient from an energy or space requirement. Doctors and nurses might communicate that they no longer use the examination room furniture because they are using electronic medical records on their tablet devices. Crowdsourcing is used to leverage the knowledge of the masses. Although this could have been done in the past with 2-D drawings, the community would have to be limited to users who could read construction drawings. (See Figure 1.2.)

Similarly, the user experience for an owner and its design/construction team is changing. The owner is no longer a passive team member with great influence but rather an active team leader that drives the team to success. This is where there is great disagreement surrounding the applicability of BIM to small projects—the argument being that it is not cost effective or even needed. The contrary is true—large projects are managed by experienced owners and team members, and BIM is used to manage the complexities. The owner is very active in the project process, or at least should be. In smaller projects, an owner's input is critical to understanding the risks and opportunities of the project success. BIM on a small project empowers owners that build infrequently to be actively involved through knowledge without being intimidated by their lack of experience. Additionally, BIM provides transparency around their decision-making process based on facts and not on the opinions of their vendors.

Communication

The need for communication is basic to any organization. All owners will say that they wish their vendors would communicate more. Quantity is not really the issue; rather, it is the quality and relevance of the communication that is important. Critical thought in e-mail has been replaced by stream of consciousness. Automated systems such as Web collaboration have added to the volume. While technology has increased the ability to communicate, it does not necessarily mean that the quality of communication has improved. With the advent of e-mail, the ability to send an e-mail to everyone on a project has crammed our in-boxes with information at a pace that has become unmanageable. BIM has the potential to bring a new level of quality communication to an owner. It also has the potential, due to the volume of data generated, to create increased volumes without increased quality.

Visualization has been a key feature in BIM that has been the basis of much excitement in the industry. Within some organizations, BIM is viewed purely as a visualization tool and is sometimes referred to as 3-D software. Early adoption of BIM was mostly used for marketing purposes. While BIM is much more than a visualization tool, it does not mean that the visualization aspect is not highly beneficial. It increases the quality of communication between owners and the design and construction vendors. Not all owners have the spatial aptitude to read plans and visualize spaces. The typical renderings that are used for design decisions with owners are helpful but lack detail to make specific decisions. The visualization capability also engages additional stakeholders within an owner's organization.

As BIM continues to evolve, owners will benefit from additional communication not just through visualization but also through reporting. The ability to extract data from the BIM database will give owners specific information about their buildings.

The tools available to foster communication are typically referred to as collaboration tools. Collaboration can have a broad definition, and the tools associated with collaboration can be as simple as

A TALE FROM THE TRENCHES

An owner received a BIM from his contractor, not as part of a requirement but because the contractor used BIM as part of its construction process. The contractor used BIM for coordination and saw great benefit in laying out mechanical rooms that had limited space. The owner walked through the model and was very impressed with the layout. The owner then had a maintenance manager meet with him to look at the model. When they walked into the mechanical room, the owner demonstrated how efficiently the contractor was able to fit equipment into the space. The maintenance manager walked through the room in the BIM and pointed out that while the equipment laid out well, performing maintenance would require a gymnast. The maintenance manager provided input that would make performing maintenance more accessible.

---

sending e-mail or posting to a File Transfer Protocol (FTP) site. It can also be as complex as product life cycle management (PLCM) systems. There are myriad Web collaboration tools on the market, such as SharePoint, PlanWell Collaborate, Buzzsaw, Basecamp, Zoho, ProjectWise, Horizontal, Tekla, Solibri, to name a few. But none of them supports BIM files in a way that is independent of BIM authoring tools and incorporating authoritative workflow to make changes to the model. These systems will start to become prevalent. The focus of sharing a model is the mildest form of collaboration, but until every stakeholder in the project can provide feedback within an authoritative framework, there will be challenges. The word "authoritative" is important as it relates to professional liability. If the twenty-five-year-old CAD (no BIM) operator is making a change in a BIM model on behalf of the structural engineer of record, it requires authoritative approval. The real-time trailer meetings for BIM coordination can be beneficial as long as authoritative members are present to make real-time decisions and approvals. This is rarely the case.

Procurement

Any BIM, if loaded with all possible building information, will have all of the specifications and quantities built within the model. Therefore, the architects can "take off" the exact quantities for estimating the pre-bid budget. With a BIM, even a general contractor can take off quantities to match and confirm its own quantities. Each object in the model can have a price associated with it, making it easier to generate a bill of materials and product cost estimates. For example, a hotel owner can have 5,000 rooms that have the exact same requirements for carpets or tiles. This can be used for cost estimates up front while tracking renovation and maintenance procedures with a greater level of accuracy.

Using BIM to determine the gross quantity of commodity materials (steel, copper, etc.) will continue to be important. With natural resources and commodities being subject to global demands and market volatility, the ability to develop commodity hedging practices is becoming important. To use a large-scale example, the airline industry depends on fuel hedging in order to run a predictable enterprise. On a large project, from planning to buyout, the time frame could easily be over a year. The ability to determine commodity quantities could hedge against increases of 10 percent or more. In a thriving economy, the inflationary pressures are passed on to the consumer so there is less sensitivity. In our current economy, projects will be at risk due to increases in the price of commodities. These price increases will not only affect raw materials but also the components that depend on these materials as well as fuel surcharges. Breaking down a building into a portfolio of commodities and building a hedging strategy may become the new norm.

This ability to break down a building into a bill of materials has many possibilities. Specifically in health care, group purchasing organizations (GPOs) have been able to create leverage through high purchasing volumes to drive health supply costs down for many hospital groups. While some aspects of new construction have been applied, such as furniture and equipment, there have been difficulties in leveraging spend in the more rudimentary building materials. This has been a challenge due to the lack of historical data and early data to predict material needs. The concept of the GPO would have great applicability to other owners as well as owner groups that choose to leverage their buying power. Many general contractors have the ability to leverage their buying power of materials but rarely pass these savings on to the owner. It is not in the general contractor's interest to pass these savings on to the owner and, in fact, would be detrimental to the contractor's project profitability.

In an era of just-in-time inventories and flexibility in both the supply chain and logistics, BIM data can be used to reduce materials management on the job site. This will reduce the opportunity for theft and damage and also streamline site logistics. BIM is used for site logistics quite frequently on difficult job sites but is more recently being utilized on more common projects that may lack site logistics challenges.

Design Guidelines

For a very aesthetically oriented building, BIM provides architects with infinite freedom to showcase their creativity. BIM also provides the ability to develop the wildest design concepts within the constructability analysis of their design. The designer can utilize the volumetric and system assembly data to analyze the building concept. BIM also increases the accuracy of the design and streamlines the coordination of contract documents. BIM allows designing and documentation concurrently in an integrated approach. If at any point the owner decides to modify the exterior of the building by switching to a different material, the architect only has to change the design and material in the BIM model. The material takeoffs, finish schedule, and specifications are updated automatically with limited additional effort. BIM does not only save the architect time, but it can also help prevent delays in the project. Because of the parametric nature of BIM, the designer and the owner have the capability to experiment with materials, space, and design quality so as to meet an owner's budget.

The BIM model provides a visual aid that can dramatically improve communication and understanding of the proposed building and its integrated systems. The accuracy in the coordinated construction documents allows the general contractor to provide the owner with a very accurate bid. Since the construction documents are more accurately prepared with BIM and have fewer mistakes or missing information, owners feel more relieved from the liability of the Spearin Doctrine (for any of the architect's mistakes). The Spearin Doctrine is a legal standard that is in effect when a contractor follows the contract documents (plans and specifications) furnished by the owner. These CDs tend to have a great number of errors and omissions for which the contractor cannot be held liable to the owner; thus, the owner is affected by any of the losses or damages resulting from the CDs.

With the advent of new software, a BIM model can be checked for the constructability of design and validation of the model to produce CDs by using software-based "model checkers." These model-checking software packages can be used to validate design guidelines and codes. For example, the Solibri model checker has several extensions to check codes for Americans with Disabilities Act (ADA) compliance and green building certification, as well as GSA regulations. It assists with validating code compliance by automatically checking the building codes. This assists owners in resolving most, if not all, of these code compliance issues before they are discovered on-site and pointed out by a contractor. Additionally, rule sets can be custom developed by an owner for any specific requirements that it may have based on its individual experience. See Figure 1.3 for an example of a model checker.

The reality is that, in most cases, architects are using BIM software simply as a 3-D drafting tool. They have invested in BIM technology for their own benefit. The software creates internal efficiency, better-quality deliverables, and an engaged customer experience. While this is a vast improvement in the overall construction process, the benefit to the owner is nonexistent. Furthermore, there should not be a benefit, considering the architect has invested in BIM in order to improve its own internal processes, but the owner is still receiving the same contracted deliverable. Architecture firms using BIM are reducing their internal costs to produce and are benefiting by

Figure 1.3 Example of a model-checking routine.

better project margins. The challenge to owners is that they are paying for a deliverable (construction documents) and are not involved in the methods by which the architect produces the CDs. It is generally unreasonable for owners to ask for a deliverable for which they are not paying. In a lump-sum contract, an architect benefits from process efficiency, and an owner benefits from mitigating design fee overages. The focus on design fees has always been perplexing, since they are a relatively small portion of the construction budget. BIM is a great opportunity for an architect to have value-based fees and improved margins. I have been involved with architects that have attempted to charge owners for the use of BIM for the same deliverable. It is simply not logical for an owner to pay more for the same deliverable, when technology makes the process more efficient. It is also unreasonable for an owner to expect that a BIM created by the architect *for the architect* has any value to the owner. An owner should develop a requirements specification for the BIM to meet its needs and be willing to pay the architect for the deliverable. In turn, the architect should be able to warrant that the BIM meets the owner's specifications.

Construction Process and Costs

In the traditional construction process, a large portion of the planning and coordination on the project occurred primarily in the architects' and engineers' minds and was not supported by technology. Hence, their decisions were mostly based on human interpretations of information generated by architects and engineers from many disciplines. The 2-D coordination enabled the coordination in just two dimensions and did not validate the space in any other dimension (see Figure 1.4). This resulted in inconsistent and repeatable outcomes from meeting to meeting and project to project.

BIM provides a much greater level of accuracy, which benefits all of the trades and builders involved in the coordination process. BIM also helps to avoid the "fix it in the field" approach. Trade coordination can proceed once the design is complete and is ready to be fabricated. The fabrication of the building systems is far more accurate after the coordination process. The discoveries made during the trade coordination process can save owners a huge amount of money and time. These savings mainly come from mitigating change

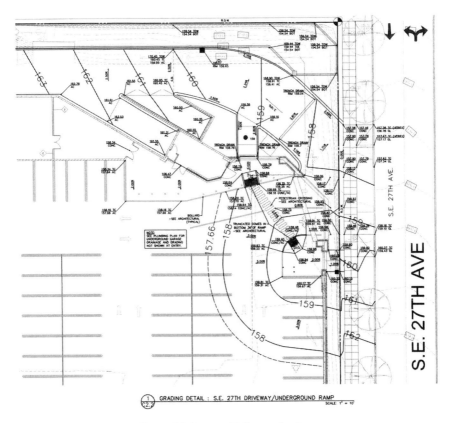

GRADING DETAIL : S.E. 27TH DRIVEWAY/UNDERGROUND RAMP
SCALE: 1" = 10'

Figure 1.4 Image of 2-D coordination.

orders. Usually, the collisions found through BIM trade coordination are found on-site during installation, after all the parts have been fabricated. Changes to the construction at this point lead to very expensive change orders, which can be mitigated if the trade coordination process is adopted up front. While many owners are not involved in this process (nor should they be), they also believe that this inefficiency does not cost them. The reality is that these inefficiencies drive costs that are ultimately borne by the owner. An owner may not receive a separate invoice for construction inefficiencies, but it is built into the price. Otherwise, there would not be many contractors in business.

Often the most effective ways to understand, evaluate, and make a decision at each critical point in the construction of a project can be done by using BIM tools. This has been proven to streamline the decision-making process and has provided the opportunity to quickly evaluate and analyze the "what-if" scenarios. A contractor that is effectively using BIM receives great benefit for mitigating risk. In some cases, the savings are passed on to the owner, but in most cases, it's the contractor that benefits.

In construction, time is money. While every owner is seeking a reduction in costs, the schedule is equally important and cannot be overlooked. Owners also benefit greatly from the fourth dimension of a BIM model. A four-dimensional (4-D) enhanced model enables a diverse team of project participants to evaluate and comment on the project scope and corresponding schedules in a very proactive and timely manner (see Figure 1.5). 4-D enables the exploration and improvement of the project execution strategy, facilitates improvements in constructability with corresponding gains in on-site productivity, and makes possible the rapid identification and resolution of time-space conflicts. Different objects within BIM are linked to various scheduling software such as Primavera or Microsoft Project, which result in 4-D construction simulations. By visualizing different scenarios, the entire team can clearly understand construction-related safety, logistics, planning, and sequencing issues. When these issues are identified, it becomes easier to identify the most effective way to build the project. 4-D BIM models have proven particularly helpful in projects that involve many stakeholders, such as projects undergoing renovation during operation,

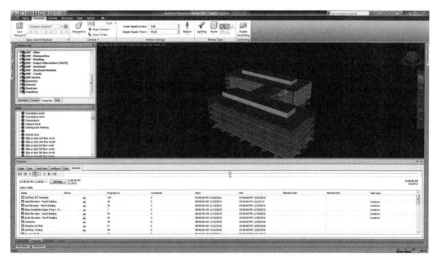

Figure 1.5 4-D enhanced model.

or projects with tight, urban site conditions. The procurement of preassembled materials can be coordinated within the BIM model using its third and fourth dimensions, avoiding any delay or duplication. This just-in-time delivery not only makes the process very efficient but also saves money on material storage, while also avoiding delays in construction due to uncoordinated procurement delay. For an owner, the use of 4-D techniques creates better transparency into the scheduling process. It is also an opportunity for an experienced owner to provide insight into reducing logistics expenses in a planned environment rather than an ad hoc environment.

As discussed previously, a data-rich BIM contains all of the potential building information, including the specifications and quantities contained within the model, that allow the architect to run takeoffs and opt for the exact quantities used in estimating the pre-bid budget. In order for the BIM to have useful data, the model must be created with the data embedded into the model. A general contractor can also take off quantities to match and confirm his own quantities. Each object in the model can have a price associated with it, making it easier to generate a bill of materials and product cost estimates. If performed correctly, an owner can use BIM prior to hiring a contractor and receive preliminary pricing from manufacturers' representatives. If owners understand the specifics of spend in their buildings, they can apply lean principles to ensure that their spend is commensurate with their value drivers. By leveraging the knowledge base of the manufacturer community, owners can seek alternatives that align with their value drivers.

Sustainability

If an owner desires a green building, energy analysis is one of the primary benefits of using BIM. There are numerous ways that utilizing BIM results in more efficient buildings. The software can analyze and help owners to predict energy cost during the early design phase, which helps architects to understand how their design would impact energy consumption and costs during the building's life cycle. Facility managers can also use this data for benchmarking a building's energy consumption. This information can be helpful to owners with the same usage type and also in the application and maintaining of certification for LEED-EB operations and maintenance (O&M).

Buildings in the United States are responsible for almost half of all annual greenhouse gas emissions, and they consume over three-fourths of the electricity generated by power plants. Globally, electricity used by commercial buildings alone has almost tripled since 1980 and is projected to rise by another 50 percent by 2030. The incremental growth in the usage of water, electricity, raw materials, and natural resources, along with the generation of pollution and waste, has left us with no option except for government enforcement of directives for building owners. Several states have already enacted a wide range of regulations on green building standards and their emendation. For example, the Green Building Act in New York City requires that new municipal buildings, along with additions and renovations of existing buildings, meet green building standards. The California Code of Regulations also sets minimum energy efficiency standards for all new homes, additions to homes, alterations of existing homes, and most commercial buildings. The goal of these directives is to increase building performance by minimizing energy and water consumption, improving air quality, and creating smaller overall footprints. The EU Energy Performance of Buildings Directive focuses on cutting energy use by 20 percent by 2020. The Energy Independence and Security Act (EISA) requires a steep reduction in fossil fuel energy use and encourages the use of solar energy. With an increase in these types of mandates, building owners are being forced to look at their building performance index and reassess the building design. Building owners are now looking back and assessing their existing building stock while working to improve their building performance so as to meet the higher standards. Along with these mandates, the government is also providing certain tax incentives to lure owners into compliance. Figure 1.6 shows a model being analyzed to meet green building objectives.

With the use of BIM, an existing building owner can make an intelligent and informed judgment during the building renovation to meet the higher standards. Apart from simply complying with the mandates, an owner can leverage BIM for a plethora of economic, social, and environmental benefits. BIM must be extended from merely being used as an information model for design, construction, and maintenance of a building to including energy analysis as well. This is imperative so owners can identify ways to reduce resource consumption and waste generated by their buildings. They can also work to increase on-site renewable energy, build consensus, review

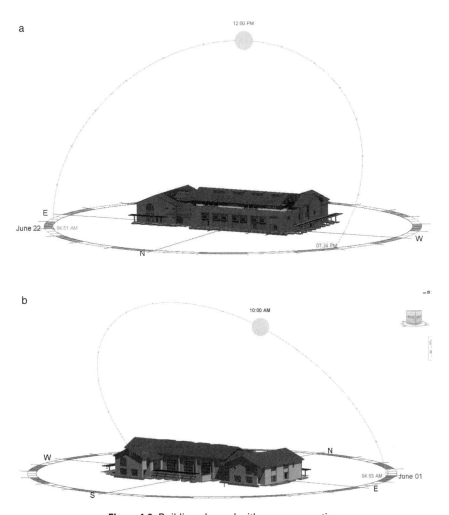

Figure 1.6 Building planned with green properties.

investment grade audits, increase building reputation in order to increase investor confidence, and also meet requirements for suitable design and energy efficiency for LEED certification.

During the design and development phase, BIM analysis tools can be used to analyze heating and cooling requirements and identify day-lighting opportunities. This further helps with intelligent selection of major equipment that meets the exact building needs without any over-ages, which reduces energy use. An owner can include the local weather and electric grid data to estimate building consumption and carbon emission while at the same time planning for long-term investments.

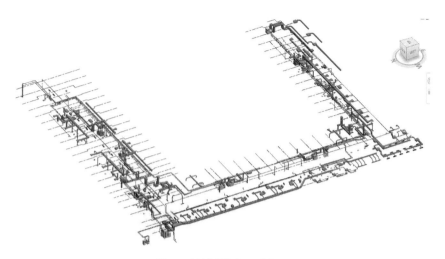

Figure 1.7 MEP duct piping.

Another significant advantage of using BIM data can be realized in water usage analysis. With more sustainable simulations, the use of recycled water for landscape irrigation and other purposes can be designed to minimize the cost and impact on water and waste-water systems. Evaluating storm water systems and simulating the performance of collection systems does not only make the building environmentally friendly but also helps secure extra credits for LEED certification.

During renovation, an owner often has to go back and forth with the architect to get the correct set of drawings; locate all the as-built information, manuals, and warranties for all equipment; and deter-mine if the correct set of drawings is being used. Then the owner is forced to work with this set of drawings relying on a best guess. This is where the use of interoperable BIM software becomes highly beneficial. By laser scanning the building exterior and interior along with all the mechanical, electrical, and plumbing (MEP) ducts, pipes, and equipment, an as-built model can be created in no time. The scanned images can then be loaded with all the building informa-tion to perform an energy analysis. Rapid energy modeling enables building energy assessments with smaller budgets and a shorter time frame. The model re-created from the scanned images can also help to screen for high-carbon-emitting buildings for achieving carbon reduction. (See Figure 1.7.)

Figure 1.8 BIM showing how an owner can view the hallway of a building.

For an owner that has multiple buildings, it becomes easier to assess and analyze the energy performance of individual buildings and perform a complete evaluation of the environmental and financial impact before making any decisions. This evaluation provides a better understanding of the performance of the owner's entire portfolio. This helps prioritize the overall modernization and renovation programs while also helping to focus on the buildings with highest impact.

By using BIM modeling and analysis tools, information about a building can be presented at any time with high accuracy. A building owner can feel more confident about its building and present a proposed modification with higher clarity to the other stakeholders and decision makers. With a BIM model, the ultimate decision makers can virtually walk through the building to see the modifications and feel the spaces. This provides them with a better understanding of the project and builds consensus on any issue that may arise. Figure 1.8 shows the virtual view of the hallway of a building.

Preventive Maintenance

An owner has more than just design and construction incentives to implement BIM in the construction process. BIM is a digital representation of all the design, construction, and facility information that is carried over from one party to another and finally delivered to the owner. BIM software creates a database that contains a data repository that can be used for purposes that vary from analysis and benchmarking to facility maintenance and management. This data can also be linked to other data or data sets for interpretation. There is absolutely no limitation on how much value a BIM can deliver to the owner. BIM enables data management of the entire building and has the ability to update and retain all the information in multiple dimensions. If the goals of a BIM implementation on a project are identified in the earlier stages, an owner can customize the data entry in the building elements to any level of development. For example, asset identification could be provided to allow an owner to schedule and track assets for depreciation. Any data regarding building elements can be entered in nongraphical form and later can be identified and linked with any maintenance and management software. The data can later be used for predictive or preventive maintenance. A schedule that will create an alert for any mechanical part that requires attention at a particular interval of time can be created. BIM can also generate as-built floor plans and elevations and produce data regarding paint colors for the accent wall in the executive conference room on the eleventh floor for any renovation work. If created correctly, BIM can also generate a warranty list for maintenance, such as locating the equipment maker, expiration date, and other information related to that particular equipment's maintenance.

Facility transition and space reallocation occur on many renovation projects. The facility manager typically works from (or perhaps has to track down from the architect) a set of as-built drawings that may or may not be accurate. The accuracy of these drawings usually depends on the building's age and the number of tenants that have occupied the space. Even worse, in the absence of as-built drawings, facility managers end up redrawing the space, which wastes time and energy in creating what would have already existed if there had been a BIM of the building. If the as-built records do not exist, dimensional information can easily be captured using 3-D laser scanning devices. Many facility managers who execute frequent moves find it easily justifiable to capture as-built information and build it into the BIM. In cases where tenants do not own the building, they can greatly benefit from the BIM provided by the owners to manage their own spaces.

Figure 1.9 Walk-through of a space.

BIM provides an improved 3-D visualization of the space throughout the life cycle of the building. The database of the BIM model can be linked with spatial management software. This software allows three-dimensional planning and can even include a virtual walk-through of a space, as shown in Figure 1.9. Owners can see and track assets through multiple moves over time. In cases like insurance claims or dispute resolution, it is incredibly helpful for an owner to reproduce what a building looked like in previous years before any remodels and expansions took place.

The BIM data repository also allows for analysis of all the decisions made in the past for any evidence-based design in the future.

CHAPTER SUMMARY KEY POINTS

- BIM is a digital database of physical and functional characteristics and information about a building that can be viewed in more than three dimensions.
- BIM enables an organization to build the building as it would be constructed on-site to help eliminate many of the inefficiencies of the construction process.
- The data-rich model can be used throughout the life cycle of a building.

- BIM can be used for creating as-built documentation for existing buildings, space reporting, spatial management, and tenant management as well as evaluating how well a proposed design meets the program requirements.

- Owners know all of the facts and numbers, yet they still accept the price of overall construction waste and build it into their estimate, budget, fee, contingency, and so on.

- Building owners hold special initiatives to implement BIM for the construction and maintenance of the building.

- Owners can protect their own interests and achieve their goals by modifying this whole arrangement and engaging the entire team to work outside the norm and under one umbrella by adopting new methods of project delivery.

- To improve efficiency in project delivery, the entire process must achieve a high level of coordination through better integration of information and process optimization.

- Integrated project delivery (IPD) is the reinitialized method of project partnering that utilizes the talent, experience, and input of all the team members from the beginning of the project.

- When implementing IPD, all team members need to think outside of the box to implement BIM to its maximum capacity.

- The IPD process is usually applied throughout the life cycle of the project, from design to fabrication and to the completion of the project.

- With an IPD, there is mutual risk and reward for the team.

- The lean process is the process or philosophy of reducing waste (time, material, and labor) and increasing value.

- Typically, the waste that is reduced in the lean process is change orders, poor information flow, rework, and the like.

- A general misconception is that IPD is required for BIM to be effective.

- The lean process reduces the overall cost of a project by identifying issues at a time when they are still inexpensive

to correct or at a time when the value to the owner can be
determined.

- BIM provides owners with decision support data so they
  can better understand the true value of a design change prior
  to the construction process.
- User experience is scientific, and, in most cases, the user
  community is fairly predictive.

chapter

2

BIM with a Purpose

When discussing the impact of BIM on the construction industry, there must be an understanding of the different uses for which BIM is being employed. There are many different points of view when discussing the different purposes of BIM. For an owner, it should be clear that a model created by a stakeholder is created for the use and benefit of that respective stakeholder. In other words, an architect is not creating a BIM for the contractor but rather for his or her own benefit. In most cases, this is regardless of whether or not the stakeholder is being paid by the owner to create the BIM. Because of this, the advent of third-party BIM services for the owner is becoming more common. As of this writing, there are four main BIM objectives:

- Architect's BIM
- Contractor's BIM
- Building product manufacturer's BIM
- Owner's BIM

Government organizations, such as the General Services Administration (GSA), the U.S. Army Corps of Engineers (USACE), and the Naval Facilities Engineering Command (NAVFAC), have begun requesting BIM on current projects to serve as a baseline for development of their individual "BIM initiatives." As with the rest of the building industry, these organizations have sought to adopt BIM standards. Furthermore, the National Building Information Modeling Standard (NBIMS) has stated its vision for "an improved planning, design, construction, operation, and maintenance process using a standardized machine-readable information model for each facility, new or old, which contains all appropriate information, created or gathered about that facility in a format usable by all throughout its life cycle."

While the building industry is focused on this BIM standardization, much of it is focused on processes dealing with the interoperability and collaboration of the "M"—the model itself. Little attention has been given to adopting established practical standards regarding the interoperability and collaboration of the "I"—*information*. This has left industry firms desperately seeking guidance as to how to comply with the wide array of differing BIM scope requests. Many owners believe that the benefit of unique or custom standards is a differentiator. While this is the case, historically industries that develop high levels of standardization typically benefit more than those developing their own unique standards. The vendor community will always build the learning curve into its pricing and the ability for a vendor to staff less expensive resources is not possible. Standardization leads to price commoditization of staffing while still driving the benefit of the technology.

Additionally, the industry has begun to realize that working collaboratively on a model presents inherent contractual obstacles for the owner/manager (e.g., government agency), designer, and builder. Traditional legal responsibilities, such as a structural engineer's stamp on a drawing, which is regulated by a state board of engineers, are preventing the transfer of the model to other parties or its use as a central repository of information. For the foreseeable future, legal/liability requirements in the building industry will dictate that contracts between the parties be conveyed in the traditional written and two-dimensional (2-D) graphical form (e.g., contracts, specifications, and 2-D drawings).

Even with these obstacles, BIM still has shown its usefulness in the planning, programming, design, construction, and operation of a building. For example, designers use it to be more efficient with their drawing production, leveraging it for improved quality assurance and more efficient sheet updating (e.g., 2-D plans, including details, can be automatically generated from this 3-D model). Another example is that builders often "remodel" buildings from 2-D drawings when dealing with validation of building alignment, identification of contract document discrepancies, and assistance in discipline coordination. Owners and facility managers see the potential in BIM for value engineering, bid package quality, facility life cycle management, and mitigation of lawsuits. There is no doubt that BIM, as is, can be effectively utilized by parties to assume more risk while reducing contingencies.

In order to achieve a more consistent and widespread adoption of BIM among owner/manager entities, designers, and builder parties, a practical standard focused on the information in the model—rather than the model itself—should be adopted. These adopted standards should organize this information by form, function, building element, work result, and product, so that each party can leverage this information to best suit its needs while still minimizing its contractual liabilities.

This can be achieved by standardizing the information into formats designed to save the state of the information produced by each author. To use a "paper" comparison, this is similar to distributing drawing information in a blueprint and not the original vellum drawing, which protects the rights and state of data produced by each contributor. Thus, standardizing these formats would allow the information to be extracted by other parties for analyzing, then later saved back in its original form—all while protecting the original information from being manipulated or changed.

A practical BIM standard must focus on established industry information standards such as the Construction Specifications Institute's MasterFormat, the National Institute of Standards and Technology's UNIFORMAT II (NISTIR 6389), and the OmniClass Construction Classification System (ISO 12006-2). It should also include noneditable format standards such as Autodesk's Design Web Format (DWF), Adobe's 3-D Portable Document Format (PDF), and Extensible Markup Language (XML).

Architect's BIM

The architectural design process consists of four phases: programming phase, schematic design phase, design development phase, and construction document phase.

1. The *programming phase* is the activity of determining the "program," or the set of needs that a building must fulfill.

2. Once a program for a project has been established, the focus shifts from what the current issues are to how the architect can resolve those issues. The focus during the *schematic design phase* is on the overall high-level design, or "scheme." At this point, there is not much concern with the details, but rather the focus is on the project as a whole.

3. During the *design development phase*, the schematic design is refined into the final design. The focus shifts from the overall project to a more detailed view of the project. Attention is now paid to each aspect, space, and detail of the project. This phase is characterized by a level of interaction among the owner, the architect, and the engineering team. The design development stage begins to solidify the expectations of the owner with regard to meeting the owner's design requirements.

4. During the *construction document phase*, the focus shifts from the design to the creation of the construction documents (CDs), which the general contractor will use to construct the building. CDs are the primary deliverable of the architect. There is less interaction with the owner during this phase and more interaction with the other consultants on the project. The details of this phase can also drive design changes due to constructability issues. It is important to point out that this phase typically results in the most tension.

From the four phases of the architectural design process, we see that the primary deliverable of the architect is the construction documents. The primary deliverable—and how this deliverable has been produced in the past—helps define an architect's BIM. Years ago, architects would use hand drafting to create their plans. This required a very large workforce of skilled hand drafters to prepare plans once the architect provided the concept of the building. The drafters would work under the direction of the architect (typically in the architect's office), first providing schematic drawings followed by design drawings. Throughout this process, there would be a great deal of back-and-forth communication between the drafters and the architect as the design took its final shape. The production of the design drawings alone took a large number of person-hours. Once the design was set, the architect would proceed with the production of the construction drawings/documents. To reemphasize the point mentioned earlier, the construction drawings/documents are what the general contractor and the subcontractors use to build the building. These are the drawings that have been created by the architect and approved by the state and/or local permitting authorities. When architects were hand drafting, the plans would be manually updated using a pencil and eraser (this moved through various mechanical media) to make any changes required by the permitting authorities. When these plans were submitted for approval, the permitting authority would require multiple sets of plans to be submitted so that each department would have its own set to review and mark up. Over time, the process was somewhat automated but was unchanged. With the advent of computer-aided design (CAD) in the early 1980s, this process gradually improved, and the amount of person-hours required to produce the drawings decreased. The progression from hand drafting to CAD did not, however, prove to be a paradigm shift. This progression merely transferred what had been done by hand—drawing lines, arcs, and circles—to the computer. CAD provided a more precise and expedient method of preparing the construction drawings, but it did not provide anything more. The key point is that there was no intelligence in the actual CAD drawings and they only contained lines, arcs, and circles. This work continued to be performed by drafters, and while the ability to "cut and paste" increased productivity, it also led to more errors. Although these errors could be corrected quickly, they began to require designers rather than drafters. Unfortunately, this new platform had limited data validation and quality management functions.

CAD dominated the software landscape in the United States for architects and engineers until just a couple of years ago. BIM software, which debuted in 1987 with the release of Graphisoft's ArchiCAD software, remained a small player in the software market because it did not have the capabilities necessary to warrant a switch from CAD and thus created no demand for BIM. As the demand for BIM increased along with the dramatic improvement in the software's capabilities, there is now a renewed emphasis on BIM. The advent of performance increases in core processing, video processing, and network speeds has driven the financial entry point to purchase these systems to a reasonable level for mass adoption in the architecture, engineering, and construction (AEC) community. With the emergence of BIM in the industry, we now have a completely new way of looking at a building. With BIM, intelligence can now be added to what in the past had been just lines, arcs, and circles on the computer (or on the page). The majority of architecture firms have not taken full advantage of this new tool. Instead, these firms have continued to focus on the production of construction drawings and tend to use BIM primarily as a drafting tool for design intent purposes. In short, the model is for their architectural purposes and not necessarily for construction purposes. This can be seen in the fact that no great care is taken by the architect to "construct" the building in BIM as it would be constructed in the field. Instead, architects tend to work with the single purpose of creating construction documents and specifications. Architects do not put the level of detail necessary into their models that would make them suitable for construction.

While this is not the ideal use of BIM, most firms lack the experience in both technology and construction knowledge to take full advantage of BIM. However, delivering anything in addition to construction documents may not be in the architect's scope of work and, in fact, could increase professional liability. The architect's BIM is created by the architect for the architect with the single purpose of construction document development. This is a great use of the technology, as the architect inherently creates a better set of construction documents due to the built-in data validation and quality management functions that are core to BIM. The ability to link plan views and iterations of details so that design changes are reviewed in real time is highly beneficial. Enhanced coordination methods using clash detection also drive a higher conducted set of construction documents. For example, look at how architects handle walls within a model. If we were to study a large sampling of models created by architects, we would find that almost every wall is depicted as a demising wall. A demising wall is the boundary that separates one tenant's space from that of another tenant as well as from the common corridor. This, however, is not how buildings are constructed in the real world. Again, consider that the architect is not concerned with quantities, but only with producing the construction drawings.

It is understandable that the architect would not be as concerned about accurate quantities, since the quantities are only important to the general contractor and the subcontractors. The general contractor has estimators on staff whose sole job is to review construction documents in order to determine quantities. The reason behind this is that the general contractor has to order the materials that the building is going to be constructed from. If the general contractor has accurate quantity numbers, then it only pays for what it needs instead of paying for materials that are not needed. This is of the utmost importance to the general contractor and is a good example of why not representing walls correctly can impact quantities and cost. Again, the construction drawings are the documents to be permitted and used for construction, but getting the plans permitted and being able to build a building from those plans are two very different things. If the architect places all walls as demising walls, it will not make any difference in the construction drawings as these are just lines and circles on a page.

In an effort to take advantage of the intelligence of BIM, some architecture firms have actually focused on the conceptual and schematic phases. For instance, one architecture firm that was designing a senior living space brought in medical professionals to help them create a better design. These professionals walked the architects through their design to give them a better understanding of how they should think about the design. This has changed the way that owners look at their projects as they are now a part of the

A TALE FROM THE TRENCHES

An architecture firm in Illinois focused on the design of a senior living space brought in medical professionals to help them create a better design. These medical professionals were the stakeholders of the project and represented the owner's requirements for space use. They had these professionals walk them through their design to help them understand what should be changed and how they should think about the design. This has changed the way that owners look at things, since they are now a part of the process and the business plan. Unfortunately, this desire to create a better design has not translated into the production of a more constructable BIM.

process as well as the business plan. Unfortunately, this desire to create a better design has not translated into the production of a more constructable BIM.

Contractor's BIM

BIM has provided contractors with the ability to identify design issues with the building before the construction trailer is placed on the site. To do this, the contractor must use BIM to "build" the building on the computer from the construction drawings and specs in order to identify any issues. This is also referred to as a constructability model. Contractors have driven BIM much closer to simulation when compared to any other group. BIM as a process has always been compared to the aerospace/automotive design and manufacturing process. By simulating the construction process on the computer and predicting construction outcomes, contractors can find problems that may affect the price, schedule, and quality of the facility. In other words, they use the decision support data to make decisions early in the process. The contractor must have modelers who are familiar with how a building is built, as the creation of the BIM must mirror the construction of the actual building. By using this method, many design issues can be identified that would not be as easy to find in the 2-D drawings. As an example, consider a building for which the construction documents had been approved, but prior to construction, the contractor decided to create a BIM for constructability purposes. During the creation of the model, the modelers found that, in this ten-story building, each floor had a conference room in the same area. As the floors were modeled, the modelers found that there was an X-brace in the wall on each floor blocking the area where the doors to the conference room were to be placed. No one had caught this design issue previously because everyone was focused on the 2-D plans rather than the 3-D model. By constructing the BIM just as the building would be built, the contractor was able to identify this design issue and resolve it before anything was constructed. Recent studies have shown that, with each succeeding phase in the construction process, the cost to correct a design issue increases by a factor of 10—proving that it is much cheaper and easier to move a wall with a mouse than with a jackhammer.

A TALE FROM THE TRENCHES

Recently, there was a terminal project at a large airport, which was a joint venture among three general contractors. As with many joint ventures, many of the overhead expenses of the project were accounted for within the joint venture. In this case, each contractor had BIM capability within the company. Since BIM was viewed as an expense mentally and overhead to the project, the general contractors could not agree on the expense of BIM and its cost allocation to the joint venture. The expense was quite large due to the size of the construction project. The general contractors also spent a lot of time developing a plan only to realize that they could not perform all the modeling themselves. The team decided to subordinate the BIM requirements to the subcontractors and trades. They did not perform any modeling and required the subcontractors to provide BIM submittals (plumbing, drywall, acoustic ceilings, etc.). It is becoming more common for trades like plumbing (see Figure 2.1) to model their respective trade.

Figure 2.1 BIM model of the plumbing system for a building.

Their method of communication was BIM and their submittals were BIM. They realized that this project was large enough that they could expect that their drywall contractor (which was not a small contractor) would develop BIM capability and perform BIM on this project. In this case, the owner and the general contractors determined that if an organization did not want to adopt BIM, then it did not need to submit a bid. The outcomes for this project were mixed. The mandate of BIM forced many subcontractors to commit to providing BIM without having capability. The team essentially learned BIM on the owner's nickel. This is positive for the industry to drive adoption and exposure, but many said that the benefit of BIM was limited due to a novice team. Many of the subcontractors actually claimed that the project was not profitable for them because of the investments they had to make in BIM.

Building Product Manufacturer's BIM

The building product manufacturer's BIM contains a great deal of information, or intelligence, about its product. Building product manufacturers (BPMs) want to make certain that architects and general contractors can quickly place their products into the BIM. The ability to execute this with all relevant product data greatly increases the probability that their products will be used in the building, thus increasing sales. A prime example of a company that would create a BPM's BIM is Trane. Trane is a leading seller of heating, ventilating, and air conditioning (HVAC) equipment for commercial and private-sector projects in the United States. It is vital to Trane that it be able to provide an accurate model of its equipment to the mechanical contractor so that its product will be specified in the model and in the construction drawings. This information is not only useful in the initial model but also becomes even more important once the building is built. The more information that the BPMs provide about their products, the better chance they have of their products being chosen for use in the building. The BPMs are also considering the extended life cycle of the building. If they provide enough information about their products, then the owner's model will contain critical warranty and maintenance information for facility management purposes. This will help the owner once the building has been delivered. I like to think of BIM as an owner's manual. People spend $20,000 on a car and the manufacturer provides them with an owner's manual. Owners spend $50 million on a building, and typically they receive a box of drawings (some of which have coffee stains on them and others have boot prints on them) and maybe a compact disc containing some of the plans. The owner may also be given the warranty information on products that were installed in the building, but most often they are not. When the BIM includes the BPM's information, or a BPM's BIM, owners will finally have the owner's manual that "they have been looking for." BPMs have the opportunity to significantly transform the old BIM (building information modeling) into an improved BIM that might be better referred to as building intelligence modeling. Currently, most BIM buildings are limited by the "garbage in, garbage out" phenomenon, where "dumb" generic objects (which are incapable of providing intelligent analysis of the BIM model) are being used. It is imperative

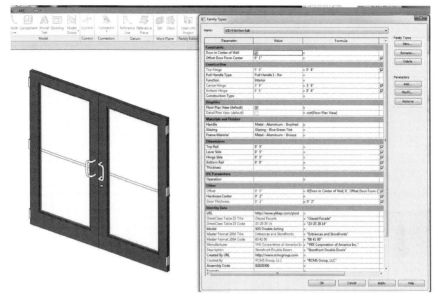

Figure 2.2 A door as a BIM object.

that BPMs share their product expertise and financial clout in order to provide high-quality manufacturer-specific BIM objects in which windows, doors (see Figure 2.2), pumps, fans, chillers, and lighting fixtures (for instance) are packaged with relevant data that allows transformational BIM analysis and elevates it to a more intelligent BIM model.

There might be a place for a simpler generic BIM object early in the design, but if the BIM model is going to be used later for bidding or building purposes, a generic object representing a manufactured BIM object contributes to the formation of a "dumb" BIM model. The addition of "smart" BIM objects from BPMs will significantly contribute to project cost reduction in four ways: (1) with the automation of the quantity survey, (2) with a streamlined submittal process, (3) with enhanced collaboration with BIM product catalogs (see Figure 2.3, catalog using BIM Library tool), and (4) with an empowered green design where BIM objects are embedded with relevant green properties. We'll discuss these four methods and show how tens of billions of dollars can be saved by adopting these procedures within the construction community.

Figure 2.3 SMARTBIM Library 4.1 screen.

BIM Quantity Surveys

First, enhanced BIM quantity survey power is achieved because architects and engineers will be using BPM-provided BIM objects. Large amounts of money can be saved by the owners, BPMs, and trade/subcontractors, because the costly quantity survey would be done only once by the architect and engineers—not the hundreds of times currently required by the bidders on the same project. Architects and engineers can then save a large portion of the $30 billion currently spent on quantity surveys for the 100,000 design-bid-build projects currently being bid in the United States each year (note that design-bid-build projects have increased in the last few years, while design-build projects have decreased because non-government-funded projects have also decreased). Currently, more than 90 percent of the projects that are design-bid-build already have most of the manufactured building products identified with symbols on the drawings associated with the building product, along with the actual model number of the building product scheduled noted on the plans or shown in the specifications. Although the architects and engineers are taking the time to choose the right building product for a given building, each manufacturers' representative and trade/subcontractor must perform the time-consuming job of performing its own quantity survey. They also must identify, count/measure, schedule, and locate the appropriate model number of all the manufactured products on the project, which contributes to much wasted time and money. When this duplication of effort is corrected, at least $20 billion of savings can then be passed on to the owners, BPMs and their representatives, general contractors, and trade/subcontractors. Architects and engineers could be charging additional fees totaling 1 to 2 percent of the total project cost, or $3 billion per year, for conducting the quantity survey (see Figure 2.4), while still allowing the other participants to realize major cost savings.

05 Structural Framing					
Assembly Cod	Assembly Description	Count	Type	Volume	Weight (tons)
05 12 00.02	Structural Steel Framing W, Wt Shapes - ASTM A992	6	W10X22	4.5 CF	1.11
05 12 00.02	Structural Steel Framing W, Wt Shapes - ASTM A992	3	W10X30	3.52 CF	0.87
05 12 00.02	Structural Steel Framing W, Wt Shapes - ASTM A992	96	W12X14	31.16 CF	7.71
05 12 00.02	Structural Steel Framing W, Wt Shapes - ASTM A992	20	W12X16	12.69 CF	3.14
05 12 00.02	Structural Steel Framing W, Wt Shapes - ASTM A992	11	W12X19	5.97 CF	1.48
05 12 00.02	Structural Steel Framing W, Wt Shapes - ASTM A992	11	W12X26	5.93 CF	1.47
05 12 00.02	Structural Steel Framing W, Wt Shapes - ASTM A992	2	W12X45	4.47 CF	1.11
05 12 00.02	Structural Steel Framing W, Wt Shapes - ASTM A992	10	W12X152	387.67 CF	95.95
05 12 00.02	Structural Steel Framing W, Wt Shapes - ASTM A992	81	W14X22	57.39 CF	14.20
05 12 00.02	Structural Steel Framing W, Wt Shapes - ASTM A992	13	W14X30	6.99 CF	1.73
05 12 00.02	Structural Steel Framing W, Wt Shapes - ASTM A992	20	W16X26	18.25 CF	4.52
05 12 00.02	Structural Steel Framing W, Wt Shapes - ASTM A992	12	W16X31	12.64 CF	3.13
05 12 00.02	Structural Steel Framing W, Wt Shapes - ASTM A992	13	W16X36	18.92 CF	4.68
05 12 00.02	Structural Steel Framing W, Wt Shapes - ASTM A992	13	W18X35	20.49 CF	5.07
05 12 00.02	Structural Steel Framing W, Wt Shapes - ASTM A992	4	W18X40	9.24 CF	2.29
05 12 00.02	Structural Steel Framing W, Wt Shapes - ASTM A992	36	W18X50	33.94 CF	8.40
05 12 00.02	Structural Steel Framing W, Wt Shapes - ASTM A992	19	W24X55	85.14 CF	21.07
05 12 00.02	Structural Steel Framing W, Wt Shapes - ASTM A992	5	W24X62	18.86 CF	4.67
05 12 00.02	Structural Steel Framing W, Wt Shapes - ASTM A992	9	W24X68	37.61 CF	9.31
05 12 00.02	Structural Steel Framing W, Wt Shapes - ASTM A992	3	W24X76	19.2 CF	4.75
05 12 00.02	Structural Steel Framing W, Wt Shapes - ASTM A992	2	W27X84	11.17 CF	2.77
05 12 00.02	Structural Steel Framing W, Wt Shapes - ASTM A992	1	WT12X47	9.69 CF	2.40
05 12 00.02	Structural Steel Framing W, Wt Shapes - ASTM A992	1	WT12X65.5	13.39 CF	3.31
05 12 00.04	Structural Steel Framing C, M, S, Shapes, Angles & Plates- ASTM A36	20	1/2X7	7.2 CF	1.78
05 12 00.04	Structural Steel Framing C, M, S, Shapes, Angles & Plates- ASTM A36	6	1/2X8	1.01 CF	0.25
05 12 00.04	Structural Steel Framing C, M, S, Shapes, Angles & Plates- ASTM A36	62	C6X8.2	6.88 CF	1.70
05 12 00.04	Structural Steel Framing C, M, S, Shapes, Angles & Plates- ASTM A36	22	L3-1/2X3-1/2X1/4	1.69 CF	0.42
05 12 00.04	Structural Steel Framing C, M, S, Shapes, Angles & Plates- ASTM A36	24	L3-1/2X3-1/2X3/8	2.62 CF	0.65
05 12 00.04	Structural Steel Framing C, M, S, Shapes, Angles & Plates- ASTM A36	75	L3X3X1/4	4.09 CF	1.01
05 12 00.04	Structural Steel Framing C, M, S, Shapes, Angles & Plates- ASTM A36	52	L4X3X1/4	0.8 CF	0.20
05 12 00.04	Structural Steel Framing C, M, S, Shapes, Angles & Plates- ASTM A36	3	L5X5X5/16	4.93 CF	1.22
05 12 00.04	Structural Steel Framing C, M, S, Shapes, Angles & Plates- ASTM A36	156	L6X4X5/16	1.27 CF	0.32
05 12 00.06	Structural Steel Framing HSS Rectangular & Square - ASTM A500 Grade B	5	HSS2-1/2X2-1/2X1/4	3.8 CF	0.94
05 12 00.06	Structural Steel Framing HSS Rectangular & Square - ASTM A500 Grade B	62	HSS3X3X1/4	6.27 CF	1.55
05 12 00.06	Structural Steel Framing HSS Rectangular & Square - ASTM A500 Grade B	20	HSS3X3X1/4	3.29 CF	0.81
05 12 00.06	Structural Steel Framing HSS Rectangular & Square - ASTM A500 Grade B	82	HSS4-1/2X4-1/2X1/4	5.91 CF	1.46
05 12 00.06	Structural Steel Framing HSS Rectangular & Square - ASTM A500 Grade B	54	HSS4X3X1/4	12.46 CF	3.08
05 12 00.06	Structural Steel Framing HSS Rectangular & Square - ASTM A500 Grade B	7	HSS4X4X1/4	0.08 CF	0.02
05 12 00.06	Structural Steel Framing HSS Rectangular & Square - ASTM A500 Grade B	160	HSS4X4X1/4	3.73 CF	0.92
05 12 00.06	Structural Steel Framing HSS Rectangular & Square - ASTM A500 Grade B	7	HSS4X4X3/8	4.57 CF	1.13
05 12 00.06	Structural Steel Framing HSS Rectangular & Square - ASTM A500 Grade B	37	HSS5X5X1/4	2.17 CF	0.54
05 12 00.06	Structural Steel Framing HSS Rectangular & Square - ASTM A500 Grade B	8	HSS8X4X1/4	0.45 CF	0.11
05 12 00.06	Structural Steel Framing HSS Rectangular & Square - ASTM A500 Grade B	16	HSS8X8X3/16	7.66 CF	1.90
05 12 00.06	Structural Steel Framing HSS Rectangular & Square - ASTM A500 Grade B	16	HSS12X6X1/4	11.6 CF	2.87
05 12 00.06	Structural Steel Framing HSS Rectangular & Square - ASTM A500 Grade B	47	HSS12X8X5/8	111.64 CF	27.63
05 12 00.06	Structural Steel Framing HSS Rectangular & Square - ASTM A500 Grade B	81	HSS12X12X1/2	193.6 CF	47.92
05 12 00.08	Structural Steel Framing HSS Round - ASTM A500 Grade B	14	HSS8.625X0.322	13.54 CF	3.35
05 12 00.08	Structural Steel Framing HSS Round - ASTM A500 Grade B	16	HSS8.625X0.500	27.46 CF	6.80
05 12 00.08	Structural Steel Framing HSS Round - ASTM A500 Grade B	2	HSS10X0.625	6.09 CF	1.51
B10	Superstructure	2	C6X8.2	0.61 CF	0.15

Figure 2.4 Quantity survey.

The money spent on quantity surveys in design-bid-build projects in the United States, at $30 billion, is greater than the approximate amount of $20 billion spent on fees to architects and engineers. Every year, more money is spent on quantity surveys in the United States than on design in the design-bid-build projects. If one were to analyze the projects being bid each year (more than 100,000), one would discover that there are at least 350 BPM representatives and suppliers, at least 300 trade contractors, and more than 20 general contractors, all of whom must perform a quantity survey for their bid on each project. With the average project size for these design-bid-build projects totaling about $3 million, and considering that 10 percent of the cost is required to perform the quantity survey, then $300,000 would be a conservative estimate of the expense incurred by the 665+ companies that must perform a quantity survey to price the job.

It is hard to conceive that there are more than 350 independent BPMs performing this quantity survey on each project, but there is an explanation for this situation. The reason that there are more than 350 independent BPMs bidding on a relatively small $3 million project, for instance, is that there are 6,000 national BPMs being represented by independent BPM representatives who typically represent about five different BPMs. Therefore, there are more than 1,200 independent BPM representatives who could be bidding the job (i.e., 6,000 BPMs divided by 5 product manufacturers per representative equals 1,200 representatives/suppliers in a given geographical territory). They are responsible for submitting a bid to the appropriate general contractor or trade/subcontractor on each applicable project in their territory (i.e., a ceiling fan would be specified by a mechanical engineer and bid to mechanical contractors). An example of the quantity survey redundancy would be that each fan in a building project, for instance, is counted by more than ten mechanical manufacturers' representatives and more than fifteen mechanical contractors. To complicate the process, each window, carpet, ceiling type, door, fan, air-conditioning unit, diffuser, lighting fixture (see Figure 2.7 below), and so on must be redundantly counted and/or measured in the more than 100,000 projects (e.g., schools, hospitals, churches, fire stations, prisons [see Figures 2.5 and 2.6 below]), wastewater treatment plants, apartment buildings, etc.) that are being bid each year in the United States.

An opportunity exists for architects/engineers in the United States to earn at least 1 to 2 percent in extra fees for performing a quantity

Figure 2.5 BIM of a prison cell showing BIM objects.

Figure 2.6 BIM of prison.

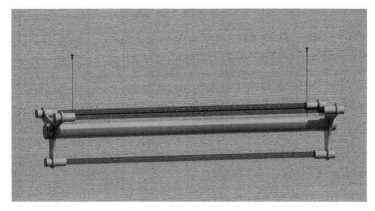

Figure 2.7 BIM object—lighting fixture.

survey on the design-bid-build projects they design. (This is the going rate for this service by design teams in Europe, where they routinely perform a quantity survey on their projects.) These quantity surveys can be done with "smart" BIM models and software. An example of a BIM-generated quantity takeoff is shown in Figure 2.8 and is typically part of an overall quantity survey.

This logical quantity survey concept has been adopted throughout most of the world and was actually proposed and accepted, in 1928, by the American Institute of Architects, the American Council of the Federated American Engineering Societies, and the Associated General Contractors of America. It was recommended to owners that architects and engineers should be responsible for the quantity survey in the United States and receive a fee of 1 percent of the project value for commercial and 2 percent for residential for performing this vital work, which would be included as schedules on the drawings. Key elements of this agreed-upon proposal, titled "Eliminating Waste in Estimating," are included in these statements.

The purpose of this report is to acquaint prospective owners and others financially interested in building and other construction projects with the wasteful duplication and consequent expense involved in the preparation of estimates of quantities under the systems now generally in vogue.

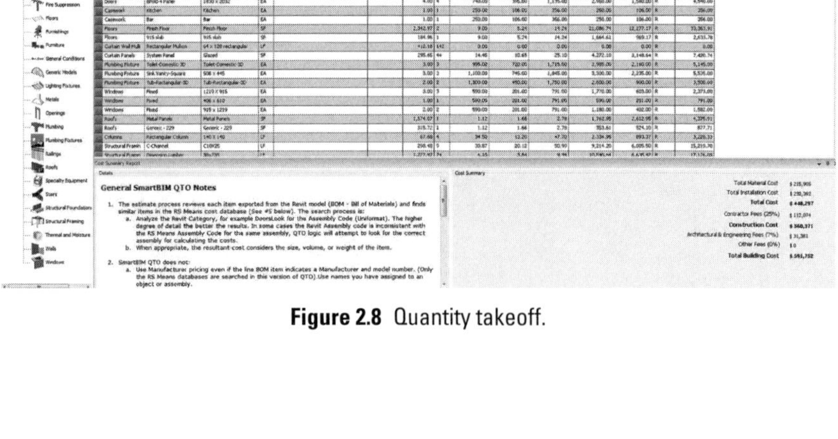

Figure 2.8 Quantity takeoff.

To ascertain the cost of a construction project, it is necessary to determine and compile lists or estimates of the quantities of materials and work to be done to which is applied a price for each item. Under existing methods, this work is done separately by as many contractors as are permitted to bid, and there may be as many varying interpretations of a set of plans and specifications as there are bidders.

To Owners and Investors

It should be noted that all expenses in connection with the planning of buildings and construction are paid by the owner. Those who contemplate building know that no one can afford to work without fair compensation for services rendered, but they probably do not realize that, due to current practices, they pay for the cost of preparation of all bids, including that of the successful bidder. Generally speaking, the figures submitted by the successful bidder include an amount sufficient to cover the work entailed in making proposals on other work that the bidder was not successful in securing; in short, the bidder's "overhead" account is much larger than it necessarily should be—and the owner pays for all of this. To eliminate the duplication of effort in estimating, thereby reducing the contractor's overhead, with attendant reduction in the cost of building, requires that all bids be submitted on the same basis and in such a manner that they may be readily analyzed by architects and engineers.

With the idea in mind of having all contractors submit proposals on a uniform basis, with some means provided whereby the amount of the proposed work will not be left to individual interpretation of the plans and specifications, it seems most desirable that all owners, through their architects or engineers, should submit to bidders with the plans and specifications a so-called quantity survey. No proposals should be considered other than those based on the quantity survey accompanying the plans and specifications. It is therefore recommended to architects and engineers that, unless eliminated for some particular reason, all plans and specifications submitted to contractors for proposals be accompanied by a quantity survey. It is further recommended that the selected bidder should submit, before the contract is awarded, a copy of the quantity survey with each item priced and separate items added for the costs of administration and the like—the total of which makes up the bid price.

To Architects and Engineers

Although the quantity survey being provided by the architects and engineers makes total financial sense, its implementation was crushed during the Great Depression. This elimination of waste in estimating through the quantity survey concept can finally be implemented with the help of the BPMs supplying their BIM objects and with the advances made with the BIM quantity survey. Architects and engineers can "step up" to earn extra fees, along with providing the much-needed quantities and schedules of manufactured building products for independent manufacturers' representatives and trade/subcontractors. The clarity that results when constructors and manufacturers' representatives are all using a common quantity survey not only saves money but also removes many of the legal and time-consuming hassles associated with bidding mistakes.

BIM Building Product Submittals

Interviews with manufacturers' representatives reveal that they spend more than 30 percent of their time performing quantity surveys and submittals for their bidding and awards process. This time spent counting and measuring for bidding projects is time taken away from their consulting work with architects and engineers about the benefits of their products, as they try to earn the part of being basis of design with their building product. Manufacturers' representatives also need to spend time with the appropriate trade contractor regarding installations of their products. Submittals include shop drawings from these representatives along with operation manuals and installation information. One of the major purposes of submittals is for the designer to be confident that the owner is going to receive the products and materials that are called for in the drawings and specifications. The architect and engineer can also examine how the building manufacturer will manufacture a unique product, so that they can ensure that it is going to fit correctly into the project. The use of BPM-supplied BIM objects in the BIM model allows an automated paperless solution instead of the time- and paper-consuming submittal process that currently exists. For owners, this BIM solution allows for an inventory of all the building products, including counts and location, with relevant details relating to performance, warranties, and maintenance, all in an electronic format. This new BIM-driven submittal process is a great improvement over the stacks of submittal sheets sent to the architects, engineers, and owners, which are typically lost or even thrown away due to lack of space.

BIM objects from the BPMs offer a tremendous opportunity to streamline the submittal process. For example, the architects' and engineers' specifications may require submittals for all incandescent light fixtures. The BPM representative is assigned the task by the contractor of providing the submittals to the architect or engineer. The BPM representative will need to review the drawings and find every incandescent fixture and then prepare the submittal package. Traditionally, this requires a manual hand count and the manual assembly of the appropriate data, such as drawings, mounting details, and so on. By using BIM objects and the BIM quantity survey, the identification and counting of fixtures can be completed in just a few minutes.

The required documentation can automatically be assembled from the linked databases and then transmitted electronically to the designers in the form of a BIM submittal. This product will offer substantial savings to the BPMs and their representatives and also provide the architects and engineers with more accurate, accessible, and complete submittals. This same BIM process could be used to advance the "design to fabrication" process that will allow architects to create customized building products for their projects.

Enhanced Collaboration with BIM Product Catalogs

BIM objects created by BPMs are not only valuable for the quantity survey and the submittal process but also for collaboration between the architects and engineers who specify and design with building products as well as the constructors who purchase and then build with these building products. Currently, there are more than 6,000 national and 6,000 regional U.S. BPMs that spend more than a billion dollars each year delivering paper catalogs and basic 2-D (non-BIM) CAD details. Although there is still a place for paper catalogs and 2-D CAD details, there is a greater need for electronic BIM catalogs filled with manufacturer-specific BIM objects. Electronic catalogs of BPM BIM objects that may be inserted in the BIM model for constructing a virtual building are extremely valuable. Also, a 3-D BIM object that is packaged with a rich set of data properties that can be electronically searched and then compared with other manufactured objects (e.g., doors, windows, pumps, air-handling units, lighting fixtures), all electronically stored and easily accessed by the architects, engineers, and constructors, provides a powerful collaboration tool. An independent manufacturers' representative often represents at least five different types of manufacturers and therefore needs a complete catalog of manufactured products that can be shared with architects, engineers, constructors, distributors, and owners—all of whom need this BIM catalog as a collaboration tool.

An electronic BIM library of different manufacturers' catalogs that contains BIM objects with in-depth properties, linked to specifications, warranties, and installation instructions (not only communicated with words and a few paper details but with 3-D BIM objects that can be put into the actual building context), offers a much stronger medium than the paper catalogs used for the last 100 years. The level of collaboration and productivity available with a BIM catalog that is less expensive (and takes less space) is a smart move into the twenty-first century for our construction community.

This BIM library manager of BPM catalogs is a software application for the organization, management, naming, and selection of the BIM objects/families that are necessary for the creation of BIM models. The BIM library manager also includes thousands of BIM objects to assist architects and engineers in the efficient creation of their BIM projects. To create BIM models and contract documents using BIM, the architects and engineers must access a collection of BIM objects that can be selected and inserted into the BIM model. Therefore, thousands of families, which may be selected from the library manager, are required on each project.

These BIM objects can be a challenge for architects and engineers using BIM. As the quantity of doors, windows, fixtures, and so forth has grown, the inventorying, selecting, and moving of these BIM objects into the BIM model has become overwhelming. All firms, particularly firms with multiple offices, are finding that their BIM objects (both generic and manufacturer specific) need a BIM library manager to bring order and ease of access. Inconsistent naming conventions also add to the problem as the same generic or manufacturer-specific BIM object is called different names within the same office. Adding to the challenge, there are currently not enough well-modeled BIM objects (generic or manufacturer specific) even available to insert into the BIM model, so architects or engineers must spend their valuable time making BIM objects for each project because it is too difficult to store, clearly name, and retrieve previously made BIM objects.

Fortunately, BIM library managers, designed to solve the problems of working with BIM objects, are available. The application can reside at the architect's office, on individual computers, on a network, or on the Web, and it is designed to collect, organize, and present BIM objects through a simple interface. This "smart" BIM software also includes naming guidelines to assist the architects and engineers in developing a consistent naming system. Consistent and logical naming is extremely important, because the BIM model is used for quantity survey and analysis. Additionally, the BIM library manager includes thousands of well-modeled generic and manufacturer-specific BIM objects that will instantly improve the architect's or engineer's efficiency in using BIM.

The notion that architects and engineers currently use BIM to create a set of paper drawings and specifications to express their design intent can be compared to an author writing a book. This process of using BIM to create the book is done in a limited collaborative fashion with participation by only the architect and engineers. The future will see a BIM model created by many actors in a more collaborative effort to produce not only a booklike set of 2-D drawings and specifications but a visually rich 3-D interactive movie experience with the BIM model. The new "actors" will include the architect and engineers along with the product manufacturers, general contractor, trade/subcontractors, and owner, all of whom will play important roles as they help to create and build the BIM model. These new BIM models will result in an interactive 3-D movie that will become a very important asset to the owner because it will depict the story of the whole life cycle of the building. The BIM model, for example, must continue to be updated or built during the life of the building. The architects and engineers benefit not only from authoring the book but also by taking an active role in the movie. This gives them the opportunity to earn more long-term fees as they participate in the whole life cycle of the (movie) BIM model. The owner is better served by the collaboration engendered by processes like BIM libraries of BIM objects that are used in a new interactive 3-D movie format (shown in Figure 2.9) that is kept up-to-date for the full life cycle of the building.

Figure 2.9 Still frames of a BIM 3-D movie.

Green Analysis and Simulation

Architects, engineers, and contractors need tools to measure and simulate environmental factors, such as building location/orientation, HVAC systems (see Figure 2.10), solar shading, solar equipment, gallons per flush for urinals, and other water conservation measures. Currently, the BIM model created for most projects is based on BIM objects that do not contain the actual manufactured products used in the real building and is therefore nearly useless to the owner for quantity survey, green analysis, or life cycle simulation. BIM software can now do a quantity survey of well-made BPM objects that can be used to create a green quantity survey and life cycle green costing.

This green quantity survey and life cycle green costing, connected to a cost-related database, allows the architects, engineers, and contractors to perform a series of "what-if" scenarios to achieve a balance between cost, quality, and green characteristics. Architects and engineers who have been criticized in the past for being too focused on design or "out of touch" with cost will now be able to have real data to apply accurate cost checks and green checks to their design capabilities.

Mainstream BIM is currently in a "BIM 1.0" phase, where a BIM model with only generic BIM objects is capable of providing adequate visualization but not thorough BIM analysis—especially for bidding and facility management. Moving to the next phase—"BIM

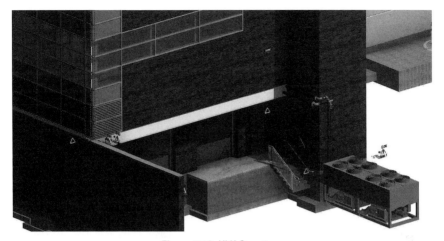

Figure 2.10 HVAC system.

2.0"—involves BIM analysis, which requires manufacturer-specific objects along with generic objects as dictated by the phase of design or construction. (Generally, early design requires generic BIM objects and then later manufacturer-specific BIM objects needed for contract documents, bidding, construction, and facility management.) If one adds the dimension of time to the BIM visualization and BIM analysis, one creates "BIM 3.0," which is BIM simulation: the "Holy Grail" of sustainability and life cycle management.

The speed and automation of a BIM quantity survey solution allows architects and engineers to check or refine costs for a project as they go, eliminating expensive and time-consuming efforts to redesign projects to meet budgetary demands. As a project changes, architects and engineers also have the freedom to run estimates for multiple design options and facilitate "what-if" scenarios. After an estimate is created, any line item can be edited manually, allowing users to input their own costs or further refine the estimate using BIM software with industry cost data and the BIM quantity survey. In order to perform these processes, it is necessary to have tens of thousands of BIM objects that are generic and manufacturer specific (depending on the phase of design or construction or postconstruction). There are adequate BIM library managers that allow architects and engineers to keep track of these BIM objects and easily access them. These architects and engineers also want tools that allow them to assess the environmental impact of their designs, especially to the degree to which their designs comply with various third-party green ratings systems, as well as the cost benefit of this compliance on a building life cycle basis. It is still difficult for owners to make long-term investments in green design, but smart BIM can help the architects and engineers to clarify the owner's decision making for green analysis.

In the final analysis, with the help of the BPMs supplying their BIM objects and the advances made with the BIM quantity survey, architects and engineers can "step up" and earn extra profit along with providing the much-needed quantities for manufacturers' representatives, general contractors, and trade/subcontractors. These BPM objects used with the BIM quantity survey streamline the submittal process along with enriching BIM product catalogs. The quantity survey is now also becoming a very important part of sustainability with systems such as LEED (Leadership in Energy and Environmental Design), because knowing the quantity of windows (see Figure 2.11) or the square footage of how much carpeting is going to be used is critical in the appropriate green design of a new or existing building.

The architect and engineer are greatly empowered by BIM tools like the quantity survey of BIM objects that have relevant green data properties readily available to be counted and measured, then properly cost evaluated because they are connected to a cost database. The architect and engineer are now ready to design buildings that could use 30 percent less energy with measurable cost savings. With 40 percent of the energy, 40 percent of the carbon dioxide, and 38 percent of the water now being used by buildings in the United States, this BIM-facilitated breakthrough is *significant*. Owners are starting

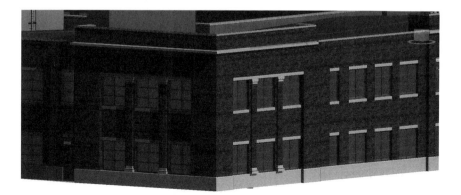

Figure 2.11 Windows.

to raise the bar by demanding high-performance buildings that are beautiful, energy efficient, cost sensitive, and meet occupant's needs, which can only be achieved with a smart BIM model.

Owner's BIM

An owner's BIM should be a combination of the designer's, contractor's, and BPM's BIM model that includes information about a building—from planning to completion and from commissioning to handover. An owner's BIM serves not only as a virtual model but also as a database that contains all the information about a building's space, equipment, furnishings, installations, and critical warranties in graphical and nongraphical format. The challenge is that currently this is not the case, and the industry is far from being able to meet the owner's needs because of limitations in software, talent, and standards. Unfortunately, many owner BIM requirements are based on this BIM theory, and there is great disappointment when the reality fails to live up to the owner's expectations.

Ideally, the architect's BIM model will be taken over by the contractor, who then analyzes the constructability of the design and adds information about the product using the product manufacturer's models. After the construction is completed on-site, the model is then updated with all of the as-built information, so as to have the most current and exact set of information on drawings as it was built on-site. The model then includes all of the necessary information on design and construction. During this process, contractors also update the model with equipment installation and manual information for the products whose information is not available from manufacturers.

The architect's model does have value to the owner, but it is limited in its ability to affect the budget or schedule. It has been most beneficial as a marketing tool for the owner to communicate to stakeholders.

There has always been a question floating around the industry—can the architect's BIM really be used by contractors to make it more intelligent and for trade coordination? Do contractors really update the model to as-built at the end of construction and hand over the model to owners complete with an electronic owner's manual?

There is a major lag between the versions of the BIM model when transferred from one party to another. This delay leads to repetition of work and endless effort. Contractors do not build off the designer's model; instead, they rebuild the model all over again for constructability purposes. Many owners intuitively struggle with this concept. This method is viewed as rework. It is not actually rework. While the same BIM software tool may be used by both the architect and the contractor, their intent and purpose are quite different.

Historically, owners and facility managers have been handed over the building with boxes and piles of owner's manuals and warranties. The owner's BIM model handed over by contractors is a condensed electronic version of the owner's manual with the same critical information about the building but with one critical difference: the facility managers do not have to sift through the piles of information to gather data. With the BIM database, any information about any equipment is just "one click away." During any renovation or maintenance program, a facility manager can click on any equipment to receive information on product, warranties, life cycle of the product, maintenance period, replacement cost, and even who installed the product. The owner's BIM and its database can even be linked to any facility management (FM) software for scheduling any kind of maintenance on the equipment or even completing the work orders during daily operations.

One of the most challenging situations for any building owner has been when to sell the building(s) after many years of occupancy. Depending on the age and its previous use, it may or may not appeal to the prospective buyer unless it can be demonstrated that the building is worth the asking price by the seller. For starters, typical buyers want to know that the building satisfies their criteria regarding its location and whether it satisfies their logistical needs for their operations and that of their clients. They also want to know if the building size will satisfy their operating needs today and if it can accommodate future growth for their company or organization. While these questions can sometimes be addressed through a visual and physical assessment, the not-so-obvious supporting systems are far more difficult to assess. Without proper inventory of the various systems and components of the building, the chances of achieving a successful sale may not be very favorable. This is where the benefits of a system like BIM can enhance the appeal of a better product to the prospective buyer and give the building owner the leverage to better market its product. The discerning buyer will recognize the true value of this tool as part of its future investment, which could translate into a successful transaction for both parties.

There are some owners that worry about the data, or information. Many government agencies are doing a great job working with the data. These agencies want and need the data to be correct, and they manage BIM as a data set. An example would be an agency that makes architecture firms model men's and women's bathroom signs and even the fire extinguishers. They also require these firms to model roof heights to a certain standard. By modeling even these seemingly small items, the agency is able to develop a library of data to use as a base building system. If we look at a typical building program for this agency, such as a courthouse, we see that the agency will be the actual owner of the courthouse and it will have multiple tenants. The protection service, judges, and so forth will be tenants in the agency's building. The agency must be able to demonstrate to these tenants what the standard tenant improvement (TI) is for the building. Each tenant, especially in a courthouse setting, will have its own unique TI requirements. An example of this would be bulletproof walls for the protection service. These unique TI requirements are not included in the standard TI of the building. The tenants are required to pay extra for these items. The ability of that agency to allocate rent is based on the base building system and the TI. This varies by department and must be tracked in BIM. The owner can then use this information for rent allocation and for maintenance allocation. The agency is very focused on the data; it is not as focused on how the architect or contractor executes BIM model creation or on how the BIM is used for design or coordination. The complexity of managing data in BIM is so important that in some cases government agencies are even willing to pay architects and contractors to attend BIM training sessions. Firms must be willing to ask the owner for this budget; otherwise, they will not receive it. Many firms leverage their past relationship with a government agency to receive funds for training. In this case, the agency understands that the entire industry is not highly experienced with BIM, and it also does not want a small group of early adopters to receive the lion's share of the work just because they were able to move faster than everyone else. Although the agency is very open, it is very focused on the data, and it cares about how firms establish the development of BIM objects and quantities. The agency standard is based on the UNIFORMAT standard. The agency does not want to dictate the means and methods for firms to execute their scope, but at the end of the project, it will dictate the data that firms should provide. Another large government owner may look at BIM in a very different way. It is more concerned with the means and methods by which firms create their model and what software is utilized. The owner is more interested in creating a library of buildings that it can quickly adapt to different site conditions. The owner also requires BIM to be used throughout the building life cycle. The challenge that this owner continues to face is the concept that BIM applies to projects of all sizes, that all stakeholders should be BIM experts in the mandated software, and that the individual utilizing BIM in the office should be that same individual building in the field. While this owner's point of view is not incorrect, the ability of the AEC community to adapt at this pace should be evaluated. BIM should benefit every project, but the extent of its use should be tempered with actual project parameters. The goal is to build a better building, not a better BIM.

Process versus Deliverables

BIM is often discussed as a new method of process. Others argue that BIM is a technology application that drives new process capability and deliverables. The BIM process is being defined within integrated project delivery (IPD) as well as within other process methods. For an owner, the only processes that can be truly managed are the vendor selection process and the purchasing process. If owners try to define processes that are their own, then they are exposing themselves to risk. Owners should focus their efforts on defining processes they own while using deliverables that influence processes that they do not own. A combination of great process definition, along with highly defined deliverables, creates a workflow that benefits the owner and drives best practices.

Many owners seek to apply BIM for process improvement throughout the entire building life cycle. Delineating between processes and deliverable requirements is a key aspect in driving successful outcomes. In developing BIM requirements, an owner must take great care in specifying BIM in a method that does not drive risk. If the requirement is too broad (e.g., "Use of BIM software is required by the architect"), then the outcome will be broad and will not meet expectations. If the requirement is too narrow (e.g., "Revit 2011 must be used by the design team to model for multidisciplinary coordination in compliance with the XYZ owner coordination methodology using Solibri"), then the outcome could be increased liability by the owner and a narrow interest by design firms to propose their services (hence stifling competition).

For owners, development of a deliverable specification is more important. In the traditional 2-D world, owners may require specific information to be on a set of construction drawings, but they do not dictate how the drawings should be developed. By developing requirements based on deliverables, owners can "guide" the process. This can include such deliverables as a Discrepancy Report, as shown in Figure 2.12. As an example:

> General contractor must provide BIM file in .dwf (3-D) file format. A BIM file for each discipline shall be provided. The disciplines shall include architecture, structural, mechanical, electrical, and plumbing. The models should be modeled to a minimum of LOD 400 based on AIA XXX. In addition to the .dwf, a discrepancy report shall be provided for each iteration of analysis in an .xls format. These discrepancies shall be noted in the 3-D DWF and corresponding 2-D views. These discrepancies shall be categorized by severity and potential impact to budget and schedule. The methodology used to prioritize severity shall be documented and submitted for approval prior to executing BIM efforts.

The focus on the deliverable requires that the general contractor follow best practices to reach the end deliverable.

Another area in which BIM as a deliverable will drive process improvement is in BIM submittals. While evaluation of an architecture firm should not be based purely on its ability to execute BIM, an owner should ask for sample BIM submittals. For every traditional progress set deliverable, there should be a corresponding BIM deliverable. For

Figure 2.12 Discrepancy report.

each of these submittals, an owner can have requirements around the corresponding data within the BIM file. It is also reasonable that the architecture firm provide limitations of use for the deliverable.

There are many who believe that a BIM is "live" and that there are no real submittals. In a highly integrated environment, this could be possible. Assuming the required technology to track versioning of data and performance exists, the real issue would be the authority of the BIM author. If the author is the engineer of record and he or she is making changes for which he or she assumes liability, then the "live" model concept works. There are many who are attempting to apply "crowdsourcing" principles to BIM collaboration. Crowdsourcing is where a group of many collaborate to solve a problem by collecting data, analyzing data, providing feedback, and so on. To have a "crowd" mold the design of a company logo or name a new product is one thing, but I do believe that a structural BIM should be designed by the engineer of record in a "live" BIM environment.

Process Guidelines

The development of process guidelines is very important to deploying BIM. Many owners are utilizing the processes that either have been provided to them or have been driven by their vendor community. An owner must define process guidelines throughout the building life cycle. The most basic processes for the building life cycle are project conception, team selection, design, construction documents, purchase, contract management, and facility management. This life cycle has been typical in our industry for decades. These processes are also performed in connected silos. BIM allows an owner to think about a building as a product. In the construction industry, we have many boundaries to manage the creativity of the end product. Applying product management disciplines to construction is possible now because of BIM. The reason is that BIM allows us to develop product prototypes that are very close to the real product. It has been cost prohibitive in the past to simulate the development of a building virtually. For an owner to dispose of historical methods and start anew is not feasible, either. The best recommendation is to enhance currently known processes to benefit the owner. To simplify even further, the *Project Resource Manual*, published by the Construction Specifications Institute (CSI), should be used as the industry standard in facility life cycle management, which can only lead to the implementation of best practices.

To develop BIM guidelines that are focused on deliverables and that improve the building life cycle process requires that a methodology be developed. According to dictionary.com, "methodology" is "a set or system of methods, principles, and rules for regulating a given discipline, as in the arts or sciences."

Following is a list of the key components of an effective BIM methodology.

Example

Mission Statement: Developing a mission statement can be an arduous process, but it is worth it. Involving key stakeholders in developing a mission statement is also important. I recommend formatting the mission statement as a series of bullet points. Keeping this under ten bullet points will make the mission statement concise but meaningful.

Improve the construction process.

Objectives: The objectives tend to be a more granular subset of the mission statement. An objective for the above mission statement could be "Reduce RFIs."

Deliverables: Designing deliverables that assist in meeting the objective(s) does take some critical thought, but solves the problem once. For the above objective, a discrepancy report would be a deliverable that would assist in reducing RFIs.

Metrics: The benefit of building a methodology is the ability to measure and benchmark. It is important that the deliverables be highly embedded with quantifiable metrics. Subjectivity is not measurable and does not belong in a methodology. It belongs in the interpretation of metrics, but not as a metric. A great analogy is in the credit-scoring business. One may have a credit score of 769 (metric), which means that one has "good" credit (subjective interpretation).

Measurement Systems: Once metrics have been developed, having measurement systems in place becomes critical. If the process of measuring is painful, then the data for the metric will not be collected.

Process Improvement: Ongoing improvement of a methodology is important for the long term. In most cases, the first version of a methodology may be "light." Once a methodology is implemented, there will be a constant stream of lessons learned that will be documented, aggregated, studied, and deployed to improve the existing methodology. Shown in Figure 2.13 is an example of a specific methodology developed to utilize BIM for constructability review.

ARC™   iBIM

Prioritized Discrepancy Report

Figure 2.13 iBIM review.

Deliverables

Developing deliverable requirements depends on the owner's requirements and varies. Factors that drive deliverables are people, processes, and platforms (the three Ps). These will be discussed in greater detail in Chapter 4. In the context of deliverables:

People: The ability and knowledge of the staff. There is no point in requiring a Revit deliverable if the team does not have capability in Revit or interest in learning. The only benefit would be to have the project archived so that it may be used at a later time for a renovation.

Process: Determining how the deliverable will be used in current/future processes. For example, many owners require third-party plan review. Most owners are not opting for a BIM-based constructability review.

Platforms: The deliverable should be usable by the staff. If it will require computer hardware/software upgrades and network infrastructure, then this should be taken into consideration. I have seen many owners brandish a DVD, saying that they "got a BIM" on their last project, but they do not even have a machine in the building with the right hardware or software to view it.

Deliverables are the most fundamental directive that an owner can mandate to the AEC vendor community. In Figure 2.14, we see an example of owner-directed deliverables that are focused on preconstruction risk assessment. The risk associated with mandating means and methods is too great under current contract documents in the industry. The specificity of the deliverables can be used to drive certain best practices without being explicit. For example, an owner should never mandate a specific software package. But, by requesting a .dgn file as a deliverable, the owner is essentially mandating that Bentley software be utilized. Without some additional detail, a vendor could create a .dgn file that is compatible, but it would not be the intent of the owner. The owner should then provide the mandate of a native .dgn file. This would then require the AEC vendor to essentially use Bentley software.

Specifying deliverables is a critical aspect to a BIM owner's requirements. Selecting a single software package, for example, will require the AEC vendor community to purchase additional software and training.

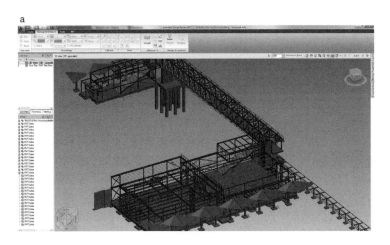

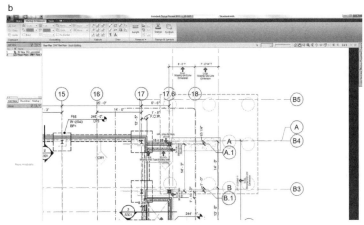

Figure 2.14 iBIM review deliverables.

This would essentially drive them to practice on the owner's project. It could also narrow the AEC vendor community and drive shared monopolies that could affect pricing. As an owner, selecting the best general contractor for the project at the best price is more important than the software that the general contractor is familiar with. Instead, some owners are selecting subpar general contractors at higher prices by limiting the bid community, and many general contractors are outsourcing the BIM component to consultants with limited experience. The owners are then shocked by the unsuccessful outcomes.

An owner that mandates a deliverable and then ignores the method by which the AEC vendor will execute the requirement is assuming unnecessary risk. In the early stages of BIM adoption by an owner, setting realistic expectations is more important than trying to execute a lofty BIM vision.

An Example of Deliverable Requirements

1. Integrated multidiscipline 3-D .dwf file
   a. Embedded discrepancy tags.
   b. Discrepancy tags shall be uniquely identified and linked to both 3-D views and 2-D plan views.
   c. Discrepancy tags should correspond to the discrepancy report.
2. Discrepancy report in .xlsx format
   a. Discrepancies organized by discipline.
   b. Discrepancies organized by severity.
   c. Severity should include a methodology.
3. Trade coordination management plan
   a. Stakeholders' roles.
   b. Responsibilities.
   c. Tasks—running clash reports, model updates, or identifying, facilitating resolution, and documentation of resolution.
4. Collision management model delivered in Solibri format
   a. Individual models to be delivered by discipline (A, S, M, E, P, and FP).
   b. Integrated models based on trade coordination management plan.
   c. Collision management methodology outline.
   d. Collision report in .xlsx; should include location in 2-D and 3-D.

These are high-level examples of deliverable requirements. In addition to deliverables, data standards are also required.

Data Standards

When implementing BIM, owners have to be thoughtful with their approach, guiding the process through deliverables and requirements and not defining core processes. Owners should provide specifications in the area of data standards. Much of the focus is around 3-D and visual representation. Data standards are very important in order to develop key performance indicators (KPIs) and benchmarking. It also makes the extensibility of BIM into facility management seamless. Data can become very complex, and adherence to a standard simplifies the process. A very simple example would be the naming of an interior door. What should the door be called? INTDOOR, int_door, interior_door, Door_INT, or would it be defined by two fields: DOOR and INTERIOR? While there are many standards (i.e., lack of standards) that can be adopted, an owner should be sure to define these parameters. For many, the focus is on the visualization of the door and not the data (as shown in Figure 2.15). Some great work is being

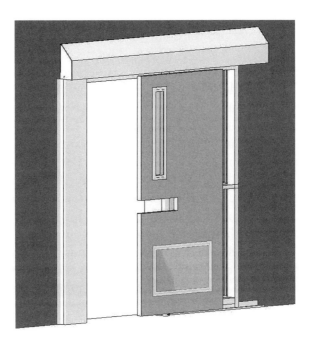

Figure 2.15 BIM object—door.

accomplished by NBIMS, and many of the software applications have standards that are out of the box. The challenge is that there is a lot of data in a building, and *everything* has not been defined yet. Utilizing a standard as a framework is a great place to start.

While many owners have developed BIM specifications, achieving compliance is very difficult. Unfortunately, the AE firms and contractors also know this, and, in many cases, they deliver the bare minimum to comply. Data standards are a great method to drive compliance, as by using automated software tools compliance can be confirmed.

Macro standards are a high-level enterprise approach to standardization that fall into the category of starting small while thinking big. File-naming conventions and software versioning are good points at which to start. We see many owners specify Revit, without being specific about which version. Clarity with respect to version based on discipline and software build is very critical. An owner may choose to specify multiple deliverable types such as Navis, Solibri, DWF, or PDF. Specificity around versioning and deliverable type is key. Naming conventions of files is a high-level view of data standards. I would argue that if a vendor cannot get the naming convention correct, then there will be more severe issues in the BIM. It is the blocking and tackling of data standardization. Naming conventions should be based on developing syntax.

Example: project name_discipline_submittal date_vendor name. rvt; libertyhs_mech_1_17_11_stevemech.rvt.

There are many paths for consideration at the next level of macro data standards. Many owners have already adopted their own data standards. These include CSI MasterFormat (or modified versions thereof), UNIFORMAT, Omniclass (which has not been widely adopted), or any other homegrown standard. Additionally, the software authoring tools come with a level of data standards. Once these data standards have been developed, developing a committee of internal and external members to review and endorse the standards is important. Without some level of buy-in from the project team, adoption of the standards will be a challenge.

The development of macro standards requires a methodical approach. The adherence to standards is rarely an indication of their completeness or validity. The lack of adherence is more likely due to poor implementation of a standard. In starting the process of standards development, resistance will likely be met with from the beginning.

Creating consensus around a mission and vision for the standard max seems esoteric, but it is important. It starts the buy-in process with both external and internal resources. Once the teams understand the "why," then there is great focus on the "what." The process of developing the mission and vision will also provide insight into the bias, fears, and knowledge of the team. The team then presents the agreed-upon mission and vision to the team as a draft. The agreed-upon mission and vision is then finalized based on feedback. Human nature is such that the team will always have some last-minute insight and will want to share. Everyone wants to yell "stop the presses," and providing a window of time for them to do so is beneficial.

The mission and vision will drive the work effort required to develop the standard. The standard should be developed in iterations and presented as a draft to the team, seeking input along the way. Once the draft is finalized, an implementation plan should be developed. The first step in implementation is training.

Training is an element of implementation that is often left until the end of an effort. Training internal and external teams on the standard and providing resources are essential. Development of a basic training program that includes manuals, frequently asked questions (FAQs), and some classroom-style teaching is required. The more serious the training program that is implemented, the more seriously the learning will be viewed. Keep in mind, especially with external team members, that they may not have the resources to teach themselves. Providing such a resource for these team members to learn is imperative. In working with a capital development board, their largest concern regarding implementing a BIM requirement and specification was that the AEC community would view the requirement as a hindrance to doing business with them. Furthermore, they felt that this would, in fact, reduce their vendor community and make the procurement process less competitive. The board had major concerns regarding subcontractors and their ability to implement technology that would drive compliance with the specification. In this case, the capital development board decided to wait a year to deploy a BIM requirement. Instead, they could have opted to provide a resource to train and educate the vendor community regarding compliance with the requirement.

The next step in implementation is the ability to customize and configure the requirement based on applicability to the specific project. This avoids a situation where the vendor community is required to determine relevancy and interpret the specification. The more interpretation that is required, the more likely it is that the vendor will lose the intent of the process and merely provide the minimum necessary to comply with the specification.

Developing a consistent compliance process creates an environment in which the vendor community understands the process and the intent. There have been many situations where owners have had a compliance requirement that changed from project to project. The vendor community looks at the situation as the owners changing their minds and does not take the requirement serious. It becomes a situation of passive compliance to get paid rather than understanding intent.

Compliance with a data standard is an objective approach that can be developed in software applications. In a situation where limited technology resources are available, an approach that is driven by human intervention should also have a checklist that can be utilized.

While a macro standard approach is an enterprise approach to standardization, another option that can be used is to develop a *project palette*. This is very useful on larger projects that have unique requirements and objectives. The data standards would be specific to the project and would unlikely be reused on other projects. As an example, in a macro standard, the naming convention of a space could be "space_name_space_type." In a project palette, it could be "department_name_tenant_name_space_type." The benefit of having project details in the data set allows for easier searching and for the organization of data based on project rule sets. In complex projects, there are project-specific vocabularies that are developed. This project-specific vocabulary would be incorporated into the project palette. In an area that will be discussed in the next section, the naming of an object and object data could be specific to a project or a project type. If an owner is a school board, there may be a palette of light fixtures that the board has standardized on, due to purchasing volumes and simplicity in maintenance. Along with the standardization of the product, there would be standardization of the data associated with the product that would be included in the object. This content library could be provided to the AEC community as preauthorized content that can be used in the BIM development. In the event that they wanted to provide an alternate, they could do so with prior approval.

Content Management

A building is an assembly of products (stock-keeping units [SKUs]), primitives (concrete, soil, etc.), and people (labor). A BIM is not that different, because it is a database that consists of various content that will be used to construct the building. The content is, in fact, the model. In lieu of managing data on a case-by-case basis and determining compliance, an owner can actually publish preapproved content (objects) for the AEC community to use. The data would be embedded in the object and would not be modified without authorization. The owner can control the content that is used in the model development without having to engage in the process. Using many of the existing software tools in the marketplace, an owner could then check the model for rogue content. The benefit of this approach is that it develops great consistency in the data at a very detailed level. The challenge is that an owner would have to have sophisticated BIM resources internally or would have to work with an outside organization that understood the technical aspects.

Some of this content could be sourced from manufacturers and modified to meet the owner's requirements. Unfortunately, the availability of objects that benefit the owner's purpose is very limited.

The Owner's BIM Requirements Document

The preceding information can be combined in a BIM requirements document like the one presented here.

1. General Requirements
    1.1. Summary
    1.2. Project Information
    1.3. Definition
    1.4. Software and Hardware Requirements
        1.4.1. Software Requirements
        1.4.2. Hardware Requirements
    1.5. BIM Personnel and Infrastructure Requirements
        1.5.1. Qualifications of BIM Personnel
        1.5.2. Infrastructure Requirements
    1.6. Roles and Responsibilities

2. Deliverables
   2.1. Constructability Review Model
      2.1.1. Specifications
      2.1.2. Submittals
   2.2. Coordination Drawings
      2.2.1. Submittals
   2.3. 4-D Schedule Simulations
      2.3.1. Specifications
   2.4. As-Built Model
      2.4.1. Specifications
      2.4.2. Submittals
   2.5. Facility Management Model
      2.5.1. Specifications
      2.5.2. Submittals
3. Execution
   3.1. Criteria for Modeling
      3.1.1. Minimum Modeling Requirements
      3.1.2. Naming Conventions
      3.1.3. Level of Development
      3.1.4. Information Exchange
   3.2. 3-D Modeling Protocol
      3.2.1. Architectural Modeling
      3.2.2. Structural Modeling
      3.2.3. Mechanical Modeling
      3.2.4. Electrical Modeling
      3.2.5. Plumbing Modeling
      3.2.6. Fire Protection Modeling
      3.2.7. Specialty Equipment Modeling
   3.3. 4-D BIM Protocol
   3.4. Model Quality Control Requirements
   3.5. BIM Trade Coordination Protocol
      3.5.1. Coordination Kickoff
      3.5.2. Coordination Schedule
      3.5.3. Coordination Protocol
      3.5.4. File Transfer and Collaboration

3.6. As-Built Modeling

3.7. Facility Management Model

    3.7.1. Minimum Requirements

    3.7.2. Construction Data Collection

    3.7.3. O&M Data Collection

    3.7.4. Data Entry Protocol

    3.7.5. BIM Data Output Protocol

1. General Requirements

   1.1. Summary

      I. The general contractor shall provide a building information modeling (BIM) implementation plan to the owner for approval prior to executing any work. This plan should include the people, processes, and platforms that will be used to execute BIM on this project. This plan should include the scope that is included in the general contractor's guaranteed maximum price (GMP). An alternate scope can be proposed for an additional fee with a documented return-on-investment analysis.

     II. Prior to commencement of any construction, the general contractor shall participate in the BIM process by creating the constructability model that will provide a wide range of information throughout the life cycle of the building.

   III. The BIM shall include building systems per the modeling criteria of this specification and model elements per the model element table to be integrated into the constructability model. The model will incorporate information from the final architect of record contract documents, as-built details, construction logistics, and sequences. This model shall serve as a method to improve coordination prior to construction, thereby reducing errors in the field through clash detection. The completed virtual facility shall accurately reflect the final as-built conditions for use by the owner's facility management team.

1.2. Project Information

Project Background:

Project Name:

Project Description:

Building Type:

Square Footage:

Project Reference #:

Contract Method:

1.3. Definition

I. Building Information Modeling (BIM): The process of creating a digital database and virtual representation of physical and functional character-istics of a proposed facility. A BIM model, consist-ing of multiple models used in aggregate, is referred to as a federated model. Models linked into the federated model are called building system mod-els; these models can be manipulated individually without impacting another linked building system model.

II. Level of Development (LOD): The level of com-pleteness to which model elements are developed. The LOD has five levels, from conceptual through as-built. The lowest level starts at conceptual then moves to approximation and then to the highest level of representation precision.

    i. LOD 100—Conceptual

    ii. LOD 200—Approximate geometry

    iii. LOD 300—Precise geometry

    iv. LOD 400—Fabrication

    v. LOD 500—As-built and facility management

III. Element Property (EP): A portion of the model ele-ment representing the material and information about that element.

IV. Model Author (MA): The party responsible for developing the content of a specific model element to the LOD required for a particular phase of the project. Model element authors are identified as follows:

   i. GC—General contractor

   ii. BC—BIM consultant

   iii. SUB—Subcontractor

   iv. S—Supplier

V. Building System Model: A subset of the model that represents a specific trade or discipline.

VI. Industry Foundation Class (IFC): A system of defining and representing standard architectural and construction-related graphic and nongraphic data as 3-D virtual objects. IFC allows data exchange among BIM tools, cost estimation systems, and other construction-related applications in a way that preserves the ability to perform analyses on those objects as they move from one BIM system to another. The contractor BIM application(s) and software must be certified in the IFC coordination view (2 × 3 or better).

VII. Facility Data: The intelligent attribute data included in the BIM model to accurately represent information for operation and maintenance of the real facility.

VIII. Construction Submittals: Periodic quality control meetings or construction progress review meetings shall include reviews on the implementation and use of the models, including interference management and design change tracking information.

IX. Soft Clash: When one model element intersects with another model element's set clearance tolerance. When clashing against model elements with the need for clearance tolerances, the model author shall set the clash detection software to the required clearance tolerance per specified requirements.

X. Hard Clash: When one model element intersects with another model element. Hard-clash tolerances are set to a zero-tolerance distance.

1.4. Software and Hardware Requirements

The general contractor shall select BIM application(s) and clash detection software to develop a constructability model. The general contractor will use 3-D graphic model(s) and associated intelligent attribute data created by this software to produce accurate construction documents.

1.4.1. Software Requirements

The constructability model shall be developed with true solid modeling with object-oriented software. The contractor must use Revit software for modeling. Software compliance certification from all providers and subcontractors will be required.

1.4.2. Hardware Requirements

All providers and their subcontractors are to utilize the minimum or greater manufacturer recommended hardware for creation of models and other deliverables.

All providers and their subcontractors must utilize properly licensed software for creation of models and other deliverables. The software packages used for this project are subject to audit.

1.5. BIM Personnel and Infrastructure Requirements

It is the responsibility of all consultants and contractors to have or obtain at their cost trained BIM personnel. They are also responsible for obtaining the hardware and software needed to successfully complete the modeling and coordination for all the phases of the project. The subcontractors and consultants must identify in writing any secondary tier and/or outsource model authors. A statement of qualifications shall be provided to the owner for approval for all key BIM personnel.

1.5.1. Qualifications of BIM Personnel

i. The BIM model author must have a bachelor's degree in architecture, construction management, or MEP-related field with a complete understanding of architecture, structure, and other building trades.

    ii. The specialist must also have past experience in modeling and trade coordination on at least two projects that were completed successfully.

    iii. The specialist must be proficient in using all the applicable BIM software.

    iv. The BIM personnel must be available for an on-site meeting within one week's notice.

    v. The BIM manager shall have all the above qualifications in addition to project management experience.

    vi. The BIM manager must also have coordinated/managed at least two similar projects.

1.5.2. Infrastructure Requirements

    i. A BIM coordination room shall be provided for clash detection/coordination meetings where all the team members can meet to discuss technical discipline coordination issues using the models. During construction, the BIM coordination room shall be located at or near the construction site in order to coordinate models with respective trades. Alternatively, collaboration meetings using Web conferencing are acceptable for facilitating these meetings.

    ii. For each BIM coordination room, appropriate equipment and tools shall be provided. SMART Boards may be used to view documentation (2-D and 3-D), create mockups interactively, archive the latter, and convert them to requests for information (RFIs) or other relevant reference documents.

    iii. For Web conference meetings, the contractors must make sure that all the participating parties have the minimum requirements to access the Web conference.

1.6. Roles and Responsibilities

I. Each model author shall actively participate in BIM coordination and review meetings as required by the construction manager. Active participation will include, but is not limited to, the modification of the BIM model and associated work as required to achieve coordination with other building systems or spatial reservations, and where any such changes shall be made promptly and with no increase in the contractor's price or time required to complete its work.

II. Each subcontractor shall provide the information related to its scope of work, as required by this specification section, in the format and frequency required for all model authors to perform their responsibilities.

III. The general contractor's BIM manager is responsible for ensuring the quality of the model is achieved as desired.

IV. The BIM manager is also responsible for coordinating and managing the trade coordination meetings. The responsibilities also include, but are not limited to, as-built and facility management (FM) data coordination and their correct implementation per this BIM specification.

V. The owner, construction manager, and other consultants shall have the exclusive right to use all model author submissions, including the BIM submissions, both during and after construction, at no additional cost to the construction manager or the owner.

VI. Each model author understands and agrees that participation in this program does not waive the intellectual property rights of other participants or other parties providing information or other products to the program where the information or other products may be protected by patents, copyrights, trademarks, etc.

2. Deliverables

2.1. Constructability Review Model

A constructability review model shall be created per the following specifications.

2.1.1. Specifications

The constructability review model shall be created using Revit or equivalent software for each discipline—architecture, structure, mechanical, electrical, plumbing, and fire protection—to LOD 300 for the purpose of constructability review of the design and contract documents. See Appendices 1 and 2 for reference.

2.1.2. Submittals

The contractor must submit the following deliverables:

   i. Constructability model for each discipline in Revit format: RVT.

  ii. Model in any of the free viewer formats: DWF or SMC.

 iii. A discrepancy report must be generated during the course of modeling by the BIM author and within the BIM (Revit) application. The discrepancies must be tagged or indicated numerically in the model that relates to the discrepancy report. The report must include:

     a. A description of all the discrepancies or missing information found in the contract documents.

     b. The discrepancies should be itemized in number to match the tags in the plan view.

     c. The discipline of that discrepancy. For example: architecture or mechanical.

     d. The location of the discrepancy must indicate level and room number or any other location reference. For example: Level 02 +24"-0'; Room DC 104; GL C-4.

     e. The report must also include where the discrepancy is located in the contract document. For example: Sheet A2.11, Detail B.

f. The BIM author must rate the discrepancy in the priority level of low, high, medium, based on the critical nature of the discrepancy, using his or her best knowledge.

2.2. Coordination Drawings

Once all the building systems have been fully developed, it is the responsibility of the general contractor to make sure that all the building systems are coordinated and made clash free. Upon completion of coordination, model author(s) must provide the coordinated drawings and model.

2.2.1. Submittals

The contractor must submit the following deliverables after all the trades have been coordinated:

i. 2-D annotated and color-coded coordination drawings in PDF format printed in 1/8" = 1'-0" scale in two sets. The coordination drawings must be signed off on by each model author/ coordinator and/or all the parties participating in this exercise.

a. Individual coordination drawings for each discipline.

b. Coordination drawings with all disciplines coordinated in one sheet. All the disciplines in the drawings must be color-coded, and the elements must be tagged and annotated.

ii. Fully coordinated and updated Revit model for all disciplines.

iii. Federated and coordinated model in either SMC or NWD format.

iv. A clash report demonstrating the model is clash free.

Upon completion, a record set of coordination drawings submittal shall be signed by each consultant or subcontractor. These submittals will become the official coordination sign-off drawings. These original coordination sign-off drawings shall be stored at the site by the general contractor and will form the basis for all future conflict resolutions. Any components not installed per coordination sign-off drawings or installed but not shown shall be relocated at the expense of the offending subcontractor. Cost of rework, recoordination, or schedule impact shall be paid by the party/subcontractor in noncompliance.

2.3. 4-D Schedule Simulations

The general contractor must submit three construction schedule simulations to depict all the possible schedule conflicts prior to construction initiation. The simulation model must comply with the following specifications.

2.3.1. Specifications

i. The schedule attached to each element in the model must reflect the actual construction on-site.

ii. The schedule simulation must include construction of all the elements in each discipline.

iii. The simulation software to be linked with Revit for creating the simulation is not restricted. However, Synchro or Navisworks Timeliner is strongly preferred.

2.4. As-Built Model

The constructability model must be updated and developed to the following specifications to generate an as-built model.

2.4.1. Specifications

i. Upon completion of the constructability review and all building system coordination, the model for each discipline must be updated per final coordination drawings and per the as-built generated on-site during construction.

ii. The model shall be further developed to LOD 400 and must be updated with all the RFIs, architect's supplemental instructions (ASIs), and any other changes in the contract documents released to date. Any changes in the product specifications or cut sheets that relate to compiled BIM data for facility management shall also be updated with the as-built as available.

2.4.2. Submittals

The contractor must submit an updated interim model at every as-built update for approval by the architects and/ or owner's representative. The final as-built Revit model may be submitted toward the completion of construction where the entire as-built has been released and signed off on by the architect.

> i. The contractor must also submit final as-built sheets (all disciplines) with all changes updated to correspond with the contract documents. The scale of the sheets must also correspond to the contract documents.

2.5. Facility Management Model

2.5.1. Specifications

During construction, it is the general contractor's responsibility to incorporate all the operations and maintenance (O&M) and facility management data into the model regarding each discipline and its elements according to the following specifications.

> i. The model must be developed to LOD 500 with the entire manufacturer's specific content for future operation and maintenance.
>
> ii. All the families must be created per the specifications and performance following Autodesk's best practice of content creation.
>
> iii. The data for facility management must be entered in all phases in three sets:
>
> > a. Data common to all the elements
> >
> > b. Data common to discipline
> >
> > c. Product-specific data
>
> iv. The owner's manual, manufacturer's Web site, and the other electronic documents must be linked to the model. The link shall be nested within the model.

2.5.2. Submittals

> i. The contractor shall submit a data-enriched model in RVT format with all the model

       elements developed to LOD 500 with in-built database.

  ii. The general contractor may be asked to deliver the model in any other format that is compatible with the owner's facility management software systems. The decision on FM software and final format will be made during the end-of-construction phase.

  iii. The contractor must also submit a digital database in Excel format or any other required format.

3. Execution

  3.1. Criteria for Modeling

    I. The general contractor shall provide a complete BIM implementation plan with requirements and standards for the development of the model for each phase. The general contractor must enforce the organization and naming conventions of all models, model elements, and element properties per this specification throughout the project life cycle, including operation and maintenance database associated with model elements for future use by the owner. The model authors shall develop the model to include all model elements per the model element table. All model elements shall be created using the correct element properties. The contract drawings will be supplied in a PDF format to the general contractor.

    II. The architect of record may furnish to subcontractor electronic information in the form of 2-D and 3-D dimensional design data. The electronic information is made available to subcontractors for informational purposes only. Neither the architect nor any other party makes any warranties whatsoever with respect to the electronic information (and hereby disclaim any implied warranties, including any implied warranty of accuracy) and the subcontractor's use of the electronic information shall be at the subcontractor's sole risk. The subcontractor acknowledges that the electronic information is not a contract document, and, before using

the electronic information, the subcontractor shall
check the electronic information for consistency with
the contract documents.

III. The model author must represent the dimensions of
the model accurately as in the contract documents.
Any dimensional discrepancy or assumptions must be
included in the discrepancy report and notified to the
architect.

IV. All mechanical, electrical, and plumbing (MEP) systems must include the ability to highlight an element in
the Solibri or Navisworks model and link the element
to the object size, elevation manufacturer, and O&M
manual.

V. Details and building systems represented in the model
that are derived from the contract documents shall be
consistent with the services provided by the subcontractor performing under similar geographic locations
and conditions.

3.1.1. Minimum Modeling Requirements

i. The deliverable master model shall
be developed to include all of the building
system models described below as they
would be built in the field and the processes
of installing them, and to reflect final as-built
conditions. The deliverable model at the
interim stages and at the final as-built stage
shall be developed to include as many of the
building systems described below as are necessary and appropriate for each stage.

ii. The elements in each model shall be broken
down, at a minimum, by building, level zones,
elevations, per the granularity requirements in
the LOD table (see Appendix 1).

iii. Model elements need to be accurate in terms of
size, location, and description (see Appendix
1). The model elements shall include elements
such as colors and textures that would be
required for the model elements to be visually

representative, in addition to being of accurate geometry, and to contain building information data, unless an area is designated by the owner or elsewhere in the contract documents to serve as a virtual mock-up.

iv. Best practices to be followed during modeling:

    a. Use model elements that are face base.

    b. Maintain parametric linkages within the model at all times.

    c. Do not use disconnected 2-D files. Extract all drawing views from the model.

    d. Use correct object definitions for modeling; i.e., use a table object for a table, not a slab object. This may result in the correct appearance for the object, but not proper model functionality. The object may appear correct but will not be adequate for scheduling, analysis, or interoperability with other software.

    e. Practice efficient and accurate modeling; i.e., eliminate object overlap, correctly close wall intersections, etc. The model must be accurate to the highest capability of the software application. Inaccurately modeled items will be rejected by the owner.

    f. Creation and adherence to A/E's contract documents standards.

    g. Use industry-accepted nomenclature for objects and spaces.

    h. Where product information is not available, these items may be modeled as a "concept object" conforming closely in length, width, and height and should be properly located.

v. For owner-furnished/contractor-installed equipment, each participating contractor responsible for installing the equipment shall coordinate the model with the vendor-supplied equipment. This is to be based on equipment as identified in the project equipment manual included in the documents furnished after bid, but prior to the commencement of the BIM coordination process. This is with the understanding that the model may need to be adjusted if the owner later selects an alternative piece of equipment.

vi. For owner-furnished/vendor-installed equipment, supplier selection may not be finalized until after the BIM coordination process; if so, supplier information may not be provided in the form of BIM. Therefore, participating contractors/BIM authors are to coordinate information provided in the contract documents, adjusting as and if necessary, once owner equipment selections are made.

vii. The contractor shall model all existing conditions needed to explain the extent of the construction work for alterations and additions projects. The extent of modeling beyond the affected areas and the level information to be included will be determined based on project needs. These requirements may be stated in the project program or discussed during the project kickoff meeting. The BIM implementation plan should define the agreed-upon scope of the modeling effort.

3.1.2. Naming Conventions

The BIM author must adhere to the following file-naming conventions for file exchange with any other participant or authors of different disciplines.

Projectno_project_organization_phase_discipline_lvl_zone/bldg_version_date.ext

10-1234_ABC_XYZ Company_DES_ARCH_L01_B1_V02_2011-01-14.rvt

Revit Architectural modeled by XYZ Company in design phase for level 1 for building 1, version 2, posted on January 14, 2011

Project: Name of the project

Organization: Nomenclature of the organization shall be provided by the general contractor after all the subcontractors and their model authors have been finalized.

Phase:	DES	Design phase
	CON	Construction phase
	ABS	As-built phase
	FMT	Facility management and technology phase
Discipline:	CIVIL	Site work
	ARCH	Architecture
	STRUC	Structure
	MECH	Mechanical
	ELEC	Electrical
	PLUM	Plumbing
	FP	Fire protection
	FED	Federated model
Level:	LUG	Underground
	L1-Ln	Level 1 to Level n
	PH	Penthouse level
	ROOF	Roof level
Version:	V01 to V99	V followed by two digits indicates model version number
Date:	2011-01-14	Published date of file in format YYYY-MM-DD

3.1.3. Level of Development

All the BIM authors must follow the level of development and model element table per Appendices 1 and 2.

3.1.4. Information Exchange

The general contractor shall provide the information exchange site. The information exchange site shall be Web based and include Secure Sockets Layer (SSL) security. The general contractor upon request shall provide an access control log to an individual level, including the Internet Protocol (IP) address by which the user accessed the site. User accounts cannot be shared and chain-of-custody procedures shall be implemented. The specifications of the information exchange site and implementation plan shall be provided and require approval prior to implementation.

3.2. 3-D Modeling Protocol

All the elements shall be modeled per the model element table. The contractor must refer to the model element table MasterFormat divisions.

3.2.1. Architectural Modeling

The architectural building system model may vary in level of development for individual model elements, but at a minimum must include all features that would be included on a quarter inch (1/4" = 1'-0") scaled drawing. Additional minimum model requirements include:

i. Spaces: The model shall include spaces defining accurate net square footage and net volume, and data fields for scheduling room names and numbers. Include programmatic information provided by the client to verify design space against programmed space, using this information to validate area quantities. Specific model elements to be modeled are further described in the model element table.

ii. Walls and Curtain Walls: Exterior and interior walls shall be depicted with exact thickness, height, length, width, and ratings (material thickness, thermal, acoustic, and fire) to properly reflect wall types and the necessary intelligence to produce accurate plans, sections, and elevations, and renderings depicting these design elements. Indicate wall structural usage (nonbearing or bearing), end wrapping, wall function (exterior or interior). Select coarse-scale fill color/pattern per wall type. Use red for rated walls, gray for smoke barriers, and green for interior nonrated walls. Assembly code parameters shall be in the MasterFormat 2004 Code/ Title. Check room-bounding parameters. The location line for exterior walls shall be exterior.

iii. Doors, Windows, and Louvers: Shall be depicted with exact thickness, height, length, width, rough opening, and ratings (material thickness, thermal, acoustic, and fire) with proper types and the necessary intelligence to produce accurate plans, sections, locations, and elevations, and renderings depicting these model elements. Doors and windows shall be modeled with the necessary intelligence to produce accurate window and door schedules. Assembly code parameters shall be in the MasterFormat 2004 Code/Title wall function (exterior or interior). The contractor is to note the requirement for prompt production of blocking drawings specified elsewhere in this document.

iv. Roof: The model shall include the roof composition and configuration, slope, drainage system, major penetrations, specialties, and the necessary intelligence and data to produce accurate plans, building sections, and generic wall sections where roof design elements are depicted. Assembly code parameters shall be in the MasterFormat 2004 Code/Title.

v. Floors: The floor slab shall be developed in the structural building system model and then referenced by the architectural model for each floor of the facility. Assembly code parameters shall be in the MasterFormat 2004 Code/Title.

vi. Ceilings: All heights and other dimensions of ceilings, including soffits, ceiling materials, and other special conditions, shall be depicted in the model with the necessary intelligence to produce accurate plans, building sections, and generic wall sections where ceiling design elements are depicted. Assembly code parameters shall be in the MasterFormat 2004 Code/Title.

vii. Vertical Circulation: All continuous vertical components (i.e., nonstructural shafts, architectural stairs, handrails, and guardrails) shall be accurately depicted and shall include the necessary intelligence and data to produce accurate plans, elevations, and sections in which such design elements are referenced. Assembly code parameters shall be in the MasterFormat 2004 Code/Title.

viii. Architectural Specialties and Woodwork: All architectural specialties (i.e., toilet room accessories, toilet partitions, grab bars, lockers, and display cases) and woodwork (i.e., cabinetry and counters) shall be accurately depicted with the necessary intelligence to produce accurate plans, elevations, and sections in which such design elements are referenced. Assembly code parameters shall be in the MasterFormat 2004 Code/Title.

ix. Schedules: Provide schedules for doors, windows, hardware flooring, wall finishes, and signage indicating type, materials, and finishes used per the contract documents.

x. Fire Stopping: Each building system model author shall model all elements penctrating fire-rated and/or smoke-rated wall assemblies and floor/ceiling assemblies, regardless of the size of the element. Further, each model author shall model an appropriately sized element representing a wall/floor opening or a sleeve system specifically tagged as a "Fire/Smoke Stopped Penetration." Model authors must coordinate fire stopping in building system models containing a fire/smoke stopping element for each penetration, with each element tagged with Solibri or Navisworks. Viewable parameters are to include information required for facility maintenance for each fire/smoke stopping element. Assembly code parameters shall be in the MasterFormat 2004 Code/Title.

xi. Interior Design BIM Protocols

a. Signage: The model shall include all signage and the necessary intelligence to produce accurate plans and schedules. Assembly code parameters shall be in the MasterFormat 2004 Code/Title.

b. Furniture/Fixtures/Equipment (FFE): 3-D representation of FFE elements is required. The FFE building system model may vary in level of development for individual model elements, but at a minimum must include all features that would be included on a quarter inch (1/4" = 1'-0") scaled drawing. Assembly code parameters shall be in the MasterFormat 2004 Code/Title.

c. Furniture: The furniture building system model may vary in level of development for individual model elements within a model, but at a minimum must include features that would be included on a quarter inch (1/4" = 1'-0") scaled drawing and shall include all relevant office equipment and furniture system layouts, with necessary intelligence to produce accurate plans, sections, perspectives, and elevations necessary to completely depict furniture system locations and sizes.

d. System Coordination: Furniture that makes use of electrical, telecommunications systems, data, plumbing, or other features shall include the necessary intelligence to produce coordinated documents and data.

e. Fixtures and Equipment: Fixtures and equipment shall be depicted to meet layout requirements with the necessary intelligence to produce accurate plans, elevations, sections, and schedules depicting their configuration.

f. Schedules: Provide furniture and equipment schedules from the model indicating the materials, finishes, mechanical, and electrical requirements. Specific model elements to be modeled are further described in the model element table.

3.2.2. Structural Modeling

The structural building system model may vary in level of detail for individual model elements, but at a minimum must include all features that would be included on a quarter inch (1/4" = 1'-0") scaled drawing. Additional minimum model requirements include:

i. Foundations: All necessary foundation and/or footing elements, with necessary intelligence to produce accurate plans and elevations. Assembly code parameters shall be in the MasterFormat 2004 Code/Title. No rebar-specific model elements shall be modeled.

ii. Floor Slabs: Structural floor slabs shall be depicted, including all necessary recesses, curbs, pads, closure pours, and major penetrations. These must be accurately depicted.

iii. Structural Steel: All steel columns, primary and secondary framing members, and steel bracing for the roof and floor systems (including decks), including all necessary intelligence and data to produce accurate structural steel framing plans and related building/wall sections. Structural steel angles and any elements potentially clashing with the work of other trades such as beams, bracing, columns, connections, gusset plates, stairs, structural deck, and trusses.

iv. Cast-in-Place Concrete: All walls, columns, and beams, including necessary intelligence and data to produce accurate plans and building/wall sections depicting cast-in-place concrete elements.

v. Expansion/Contraction Joints: Joints shall be accurately depicted per the specifications.

vi. Stairs: The structural model shall include all necessary openings and framing members for stair systems, including necessary intelligence to produce accurate plans and building/wall sections depicting stair design elements.

vii.Shafts and Pits: The structural model shall include all necessary shafts, pits, and openings, including necessary intelligence and data to produce accurate plans and building/wall sections depicting these design elements. Specific model elements to be modeled are further described in the model element table.

3.2.3. Mechanical Modeling

The mechanical building system model may vary in level of development for individual model elements, but at a minimum must include all features that would be included on a quarter inch (1/4" = 1'-0") scaled drawing. Additional minimum model requirements include:

i. HVAC: All necessary heating, ventilating, air-conditioning, and specialty equipment, including air distribution ducts for supply, return, and ventilation and exhaust ducts, including control systems, registers, diffusers, grills, access doors, and hydronic baseboards, with necessary intelligence and data to produce accurate plans, elevations, building/wall sections, and schedules. All piping larger than 1.5" in diameter shall be modeled. Assembly code parameters shall be in the MasterFormat 2004 Code/Title.

ii. Mechanical Piping: All necessary piping and fixture layouts and related equipment, including necessary intelligence and data to produce accurate plans, elevations, building/wall sections, and schedules. All piping larger than 1.5" in diameter shall be modeled. Assembly code parameters shall be in the MasterFormat 2004 Code/Title.

iii. Equipment Clearances: All HVAC and piping equipment clearances shall be modeled for use in interference checking and maintenance access requirements. Clearance zones for access, service space requirements, gauge reading, valve clearances, and other operational clearances must be modeled as part of the plumbing and fire protection system and checked for conflicts with other elements. These clearance zones should be modeled as invisible solids within the object.

3.2.4. Electrical Modeling

i. Elevator Equipment: The model shall include the necessary equipment and control system, including necessary intelligence and data to produce accurate plans, sections, and elevations depicting these model elements.

ii. Electrical/Telecommunications: The electrical building system model may vary in level of development for individual model elements, but at a minimum must include all features that would be included on a quarter inch (1/4" = 1'-0") scaled drawing.

iii. Interior Electrical Power and Lighting: All necessary interior electrical components (i.e., lighting, receptacles, special- and general-purpose power receptacles, lighting fixtures, panel boards, and control systems), including necessary intelligence to produce accurate plans, details, and schedules. Cable tray routing shall be modeled without detail of cable contents. Lighting and power built into furniture/equipment shall be modeled. Specific model elements to be modeled are further described in the model element table.

iv. Special Electrical Systems: All necessary special electrical components (i.e., security, mass notification, public address, nurse call and other special occupancies, and control systems), including necessary intelligence to produce accurate plans, details, and schedules. Assembly code parameters shall be in the MasterFormat 2004 Code/Title.

v. Grounding Systems: All necessary grounding components (i.e., lightning protection systems, static grounding systems, communications grounding systems, bonding), including necessary intelligence to produce accurate plans, details, and schedules. Assembly code parameters shall be in the MasterFormat 2004 Code/Title.

vi. Communications: All existing and new communications service controls and connections, both above ground and underground with necessary intelligence to produce accurate plans, details, and schedules. Cable tray routing shall be modeled without detail of cable contents. Communications conduit larger than 1.5^2 in diameter shall be modeled. Assembly code parameters shall be in the MasterFormat 2004 Code/Title.

vii. Exterior Building Lighting: All necessary exterior lighting with necessary intelligence to produce accurate plans, elevations, and schedules. The exterior building lighting model shall include all necessary lighting, relevant existing and proposed support utility lines, and equipment required with necessary intelligence to produce accurate plans, details, and schedules. Assembly code parameters shall be in the MasterFormat 2004 Code/Title.

viii. Equipment Clearances: All lighting and communications equipment clearances and no-fly zones shall be modeled for use in interference management and maintenance access requirements. Assembly code parameters shall be in the MasterFormat 2004 Code/Title.

3.2.5. Plumbing Modeling

Plumbing: All necessary plumbing piping and fixture layouts, floor and area drains, access doors, and related equipment, including necessary intelligence and data to produce accurate plans, elevations, building/wall sections, riser diagrams, and schedules. All piping larger than 1.5^2 in diameter shall be modeled. Specific model elements to be modeled are further described in the model element table.

    i. Equipment Clearances: All plumbing equipment clearances shall be modeled for use in interference checking and maintenance access requirements.

3.2.6. Fire Protection Modeling

Fire Protection: The fire protection system model may vary in level of detail for individual elements, but at a minimum must include all features that would be included on a quarter inch (1/4" = 1'-0") scaled drawing. Additional minimum model requirements include:

    i. Fire Protection System: All relevant fire protection components (i.e., branch piping, sprinkler heads, fittings, drains, pumps, tanks, sensors, control panels, access doors) with necessary intelligence to produce accurate plans, elevations, building/wall sections, riser diagrams, and schedules. All fire protection piping shall be modeled. Specific model elements to be modeled are further described in the model element table.

    ii. Fire Alarms: All fire alarm/mass notification devices and detection systems shall be indicated with necessary intelligence to produce accurate plans depicting them. Specific model elements to be modeled are further described in the model element table.

3.2.7. Specialty Equipment Modeling

    i. Specialty modeling shall include, but is not limited to, food service planning, medical planning, library planning, audiovisual/communications, exhibit design, and safety and security planning and shall use BIM-authoring software or discipline specialty 3-D software. Models shall be created that include all geometry, physical characteristics, and product data needed to describe the design and construction work. Drawings and schedules required for assessment, review, bidding, and construction shall be extractions from this model. Software shall be capable of interfacing with the BIM-authored software. In all cases, model elements to a level that allows the team to verify clearances, analyze conflicts/clashes, and properly coordinate the work with all other aspects of the project. Assembly code parameters shall be in the MasterFormat 2004 Code/Title. Specific model elements to be modeled are further described in the model element table.

ii. Clearance zones for access, door swings, service space requirements, controls, gauge reading, and other operational clearances must be modeled as part of the equipment and checked for conflicts with other elements.

3.3. 4-D BIM Protocol

The model(s) shall incorporate "4-D" scheduling simulations that can be linked to Primavera or Microsoft Project schedule-type software to depict the project site, topography, roads, pedestrian walkways, construction of foundations, shell structure, and building exterior skin. The 4-D simulation will serve as an advanced means of providing a visual description and simulation of the construction schedule for periodic review by the owner. Simulation software such as, but not limited to, Synchro or Navisworks Timeliner shall be used to develop the simulation. The simulation shall show planned construction activities and sequences, including crane and major equipment placement, progressing on a weekly basis. It is expected that the 4-D schedule simulation will be developed when the model(s) is complete, updated at 100 percent construction documents, and updated one month before foundations begin. A total of three simulations shall be required.

3.4. Model Quality Control Requirements

i. Prior to the project kickoff meeting, the general contractor must submit a BIM quality control process document. This shall address the methods that shall

be employed to meet the requirements in this specification. The document should specifically communicate the processes, methodologies, and technology
that will be deployed.

ii. The BIM author shall model to the manufacturer's
product specifications for quality assurance and
accuracy. All manufacturers' specifications, including exact dimensions and sizes, shall be included
in the structural, architectural, and MEP model
elements.

iii. The general contractor's BIM manager shall select a
common reference point before any modeling development begins. The recommended reference point
for all models should be (0, 0, 0). Elevate the model
to the contract documents finish floor elevations so
that model elements are at the correct height above
the finish floor.

iv. The model authors must clean up the model and
remove any "scratch" work, including unnecessary
backgrounds, before submitting or exchanging the
files with other model authors.

v. Any specific notes pertinent to the drawings shall be
incorporated into the model on a separate layer or
the system models shall be prepared using software
that allows 2-D drawings/sheets to be extracted
from the model so that production of these sheets
does not require a special or duplicated CAD effort.

3.5. BIM Trade Coordination Protocol

3.5.1. Coordination Kickoff

The BIM implementation plan to be submitted at
the start of the BIM kickoff meeting must include a trade
coordination management plan. The general contractor's
BIM manager shall conduct a coordination kickoff meeting with all the subcontractors and model authors involved.
The kickoff meeting must address contract requirements,
coordination process schedule, standard detail revisions,
establishment of key coordination variables (background
use and updates, model origin, units of measure, layers and

color assignments, upload time, system priority, clearance and accessibility requirements, use of halos, and approach to implement clash detection through the software program), roles and responsibilities, file management, and ceiling heights. The owner is requiring that the general contractor utilize BIM technology for demonstrating the coordination of the building systems. The owner is to be provided coordination information but is not assuming any liability or instruction for coordination.

3.5.2. Coordination Schedule

The general contractor's BIM manager shall prepare and maintain a preconstruction model coordination schedule with coordination submittal milestones that meet the overall construction schedule. The general contractor's BIM manager shall obtain input from all consultants and subcontractors participating in the modeling process to ensure that a realistic and mutually agreed-upon preconstruction schedule is achieved. Coordination drawing development, coordination submittal drawing submission, review by architect of record, fabrication duration, and delivery lead times will need to be included in a manner that supports the project construction schedule.

3.5.3. Coordination Protocol

i. The BIM manager shall have the lead responsibility to produce a weekly updated and combined Solibri model. Clash detection meetings will be held each week to identify and resolve spatial interferences. These weekly meetings will be facilitated by the general contractor's BIM manager and all MEP qualified subcontractor BIM specialists to locate all trade interferences and resolve conflict resolution.

ii. Building System Priority: The following provides the priority of building systems for the coordination process. This list is in descending order and is the precedence assigned the work items for space priority. Conflicts in priority requirements, including contract exceptions, will be resolved by the BIM manager. Exceptions to the priority listing include gravity flow requirements for plumbing waste and roof drainage and owner-dictated access requirements.

a. Recessed light fixtures and supports
b. Equipment location and access
c. Pneumatic tube and material conveying systems
d. Overhead miscellaneous steel supports
e. Plumbing waste and roof drainage
f. Ductwork
g. Fire protection (sprinkler system)
h. HVAC piping
i. Plumbing vent, supply, and medical gas piping
j. Electrical conduit and cable tray
k. Seismic bracing
l. Sleeves through rated partitions
m. Rated, acoustic, and nonrated partitions with specific focus on top of wall, "king studs," headers, openings, and in-wall bracing, backing, and penetrations
n. Above-ceiling bracing for drywall partitions
o. Soffit, hard-lid, stepped, or sloped ceiling typically constructed from metal stud and gypsum
p. Ceiling seismic bracing
q. Controls
r. Casework
s. Sleeve, core drill, and block out layout drawings. Drawings showing proposed locations and sizes of sleeves, core drills, blockouts, and embedded items in concrete walls, columns, floors, and beams
t. Priority of systems for exterior enclosure.

    iii. For each coordination meeting, a clash report must be produced using clash detection software. The clash report must include:

        a. Location of the clash

        b. Description of the clash—with discipline

        c. Picture of the clash

        d. Which team is responsible for resolving the clash

        e. Proposed solution

    iv. The BIM coordination must record all the resolutions discussed in the meeting.

    v. All the records must be submitted at the end of the coordination for future reference on cost and time savings.

3.5.4. File Transfer and Collaboration

The general contractor shall provide guidelines for file transfer included in the BIM implementation plan. It is the responsibility of the general contractor to set up an electronic File Transfer Protocol (FTP) site and provide each participant with an access ID and password.

The naming convention discussed earlier shall strictly be adhered to.

3.6. As-Built Modeling

The constructability model shall be updated as built (as available) to LOD 400. The contractor shall submit a plan to the owner for review, prior to the start of construction, that outlines the process for concurrent as-built documentation. Concurrency is mandated. Methods for recording as-built information are left to the discretion of the contractor.

In this phase, the BIM manager must start collecting O&M information to be implemented in the model.

3.7. Facility Management Model

3.7.1. Minimum Requirements

The data for facility management must be entered in phases as the model progresses. The minimum requirements for entering the data must include, but are not limited to:

I. Phase 1—Design: Data common to all the elements irrespective of its discipline or any other specifics.

   i. Physical properties of the elements

      a. Facility ID

      b. Facility name

      c. Facility description

      d. Dimensional properties

   ii. Spatial location of the elements

      a. Zone/space name

      b. Zone/space number

      c. Room name

      d. Room number

      e. Floor ID

      f. Floor name

      g. Floor description

      h. Floor elevation, height

   iii. Space compliance/validation

      a. Gross area

      b. Tenant area

      c. Area validation

   iv. Building code validation

      a. LEED data

      b. Applicable building codes

      c. Fire rating

II. Phase 2—Construction: Data common to specific discipline as available during construction and as-built phase.

   i. Component/product ID and description per manufacturer's specifications

      a. Component ID

      b. Component name

      c. Component description

      d. Attributes

      e. Maker name

      f. Manufacturer

      g. Serial number

      h. MasterFormat number

      i. Model number

      j. Order number

      k. Product ID

      l. Product name

      m. Production year

      n. Accessories

  ii. Manufacturer's specifications for product or element material

      a. Material ID

      b. Material ID list

      c. Material name

      d. Material description

      e. System ID

      f. System function

      g. System name

      h. System description

  iii. Construction sequence and logistics

      a. Transmittal ID list, information, and description

      b. Action ID, code, and description

      c. Task ID, name, and description

  iv. Installation information

      a. Installation ID list

      b. Installation name

      c. Installation manufacturer

      d. Installation model

      e. Installation serial number

      f. Installation tag number

      g. Installation description

     v. Product O&M information: warranty, guaranty, cost
- a. Product type
- b. Discipline
- c. Replacement cost
- d. Expected life
- e. Document ID and list
- f. Document name, directory, file name, type
- g. Manual ID
- h. Manual name and description
- i. Guarantor ID list
- j. Warranty ID
- k. Warrantor name and description
- l. Warranty start and end
- m. Spare ID, type
- n. Spare provider ID list
- o. Spare set ID
- p. Spare name and number
- q. Spare description
- r. Suppliers
- s. Instruction ID
- t. Instruction name
- u. Instruction description

    vi. Commissioning information
- a. Test ID
- b. Test name and description
- c. Certification ID
- d. Certification name and description
- e. Start-up and Shut-down task ID
- f. Emergency task ID

III. Phase 3—Owner's Occupancy (Facility Management): Data common to individual products and their management and maintenance that include, but are not limited to,

    i. Contact information for all the contractors, manufacturers, vendors, installers, internal FM team

        a. Contact name, address, phone number, e-mail

        b. Company

        c. Department

   ii. Asset management

        a. Product ID and name

        b. Serial number

        c. Bar code/asset tags

        d. Annual maintenance cost

        e. LEED-related data

        f. Servicer

  iii. Preventive maintenance

        a. Product ID

        b. Maintenance schedule, frequency

        c. Resources assigned

  iv. Product-specific information

        a. Example: wattage, power consumption

3.7.2. Construction Data Collection

The construction specification data must strictly adhere to the overall construction specifications. The BIM manager must ensure that all the information is correct and up-to-date. In case the architect changes any product or related specifications, it is the responsibility of the general contractor to inform the BIM manager and provide the updated set.

3.7.3. O&M Data Collection

As the construction progresses, the general contractor must collect the installed product manuals and O&M data and submit them with each set of as-builts released. The BIM manager shall follow the owner's requirements, which will be released in detail during the construction phase. It is the responsibility of the BIM manager to gather all required information for the general contractor.

3.7.4. Data Entry Protocol

A specialized Excel spreadsheet will be provided to the general contractor. All product information shall be input into the spreadsheet. The spreadsheet contains field validation rules. Data shall be input so as to not violate these rules.

3.7.5. BIM Data Output Protocol

BIM data shall be provided in the native file format of the corresponding deliverables. Additionally, IFC files shall be provided. All data shall be documented and any data schema shall be provided for any linked files or linked data sets.

Chapter Summary Key Points

- For an owner, it should be clear that a model created by a stakeholder is created for that respective stakeholder.
- The four phases of the architectural design process are the programming phase, schematic design phase, design development phase, and construction document phase.
- The programming phase is the activity of determining the "program," or set of needs that a building must fulfill.
- The schematic design phase focuses on the overall high-level design, or "scheme."
- During the design development phase, the schematic design is refined into the final design.
- The construction document phase shifts the focus from design to the creation of the construction documents that will be used by the general contractor to construct the building.
- BIM has provided contractors with the ability to identify design issues with the building before the construction trailer is even placed on the site.
- Contractors have driven BIM much closer to simulation than any other group.
- By building the BIM as the building would be built, the contractor is able to identify and resolve design issues before anything is constructed.
- The building product manufacturer's BIM contains a great deal of information, or intelligence, about its product.

- The more information BPMs provide on their products, the better chance they have of their products being chosen for use in the building.

- Enhanced BIM quantity survey power is achieved because architects and engineers will be using manufacturer-provided BIM objects.

- It should be realized that all the expenses in connection with the planning of buildings and construction are paid by the owner.

- BIM objects created by the BPMs are not only valuable for the quantity survey and the submittal process but also for collaboration between the architects and engineers who spec- ify design with building products and the constructors who purchase and then build with the building products.

- The BIM library manager of BPM catalogs is a software application for the organization, management, naming, and selection of the BIM objects/families that are necessary for the creation of BIM building models.

- An owner's BIM should be the combination of designer, con- tractor, and BPM's model that includes information about a building from planning to completion and from commission- ing to hand over.

3

BIM—The Paradigm Shift

A paradigm shift, also known as revolutionary science, is a term that was first introduced in 1962 by Thomas Kuhn in his book *The Structure of Scientific Revolutions*. Kuhn used this term to describe a major shift in the basic assumptions within the prevailing theory of science, which is in contrast to his idea of normal science. The term "paradigm shift" as a change in a fundamental model of events has since become widely applied to many other areas of human experience. This occurred even though Kuhn attempted to restrict the use of the term to the hard sciences.

In recent years, the term has become a part of the marketing vocabulary, emerging as a buzzword. In this marketing lexicon, paradigm shift has come to represent a radical change in personal beliefs and complex systems or organizations that replace a former way of thinking or organizing with a radically different way of thinking or organizing. A paradigm shift is a process of taking what one knows and starting over. According to Kuhn, "a shift in paradigm alters the fundamental concepts underlying research and inspires new standards of evidence, new research techniques, and new pathways of theory and experiment that are radically incommensurate with the old ones."[1] Although Kuhn's reference was science, these shifts in paradigms apply to other disciplines as well. In the paradigm shift, everything changes from what was known before. BIM is a paradigm shift. Additionally, a paradigm shift occurs when the new concept effectuates change in every functional aspect of a business. For many in the industry that have been early adopters of BIM, the early impact was on information technology (IT) and human resources (HR). The realization that BIM was a paradigm shift only came about after extensive adoption. BIM affects all functional areas of a business.

BIM is now changing everything in our industry. We now see architects using BIM in their practices as well as general contractors using BIM because an owner has required it. General contractors are also using BIM for constructability purposes. As BIM spreads throughout the architecture, engineering, and construction (AEC) industry, architects are not having problems implementing BIM, but they are having difficulties figuring out how to charge for BIM. To date, architects are not charging any differently for these services. The reason behind this is that, from the owner's point of view, the architects are not providing anything new.

BIM is affecting the functional aspects of the design process. Designers are using BIM as a means to get to the construction documents. For this reason, the owner sees no reason to pay more for the construction documents than it did with computer-aided design (CAD). In fact, if a survey of architects were carried out, it would show that they are doing a lot more work using BIM to get to a 30 percent design development (DD) set than they were using CAD. The reason behind the increase in time for architects to provide the 30 percent DD set using BIM is because when an architect is using AutoCAD, the amount of work starts off small and gradually increases as the project progresses. Since there is no intelligence in the AutoCAD file, there is not as much information in the drawings at the DD phase as there is at the construction documents (CD) phase.

BIM is affecting the functional aspects of finance. With BIM, a majority of the work is done at the beginning of the project as the architects set up families and create content to be included in the model. This is a result of their performing a great deal more work up front to get that 30 percent DD set delivered. Architects are faced with two problems, the first being that they are still billing their clients according to the pre-BIM terms. Consequently, this means that they do a substantial amount of up-front BIM work but cannot bill it until later in the process. The second is that architects need to develop a new deliverable for which they can charge the owner. Currently, architects cannot charge more for BIM because the owner is not concerned with how the architect creates the CDs. BIM is not seen by the owner as a reason for the architect to charge more for the drawings, and this is a problem for the architect. Owners are more concerned with getting the best price than with how the CDs are created. If architects try to charge extra based on the fact that they are using BIM on the project, they will have to have a justification for the additional cost. The architects cannot respond by saying BIM will help them create a better design because then the owner will ask about the product the architect had been providing in the past. This inability to charge extra for BIM on services that architects already provide has become a major problem, as it is affecting the finances and cash flow of many architecture firms. One possible solution to this would be for architecture firms to provide a model to the owner that could be used for facility management. This would require incorporating all of the as-built changes into the model as well as all of the subcontractor models, but, at the same time, it would provide the owner with a model that could be used for maintenance and future build-outs. This would require a change in the way that architects create their BIM models, or it could be an opportunity for them to outsource their modeling to a third-party provider that could create and maintain the model and leave the architects free to do what they do best—design.

BIM is affecting the functional aspects of the IT department. To be effective and efficient in BIM, an organization must have the most up-to-date hardware and software. This requires updating desktop workstations and laptops every year to take full advantage of an organization's BIM capabilities. Unfortunately, the IT issues are not limited to just desktop workstations and laptops. BIM IT needs include servers and entire networks as well. Because BIM software is such a memory and storage space "hog," an organization must purchase very powerful servers to handle the memory needs and must also buy larger storage devices to hold the ever-increasing BIM file sizes (some single files can exceed 300 MB). In addition to the servers, an organization will also need to purchase backup hardware and software to protect against a catastrophic loss of data. Beyond the hardware costs lie the software costs. For most BIM software applications, there is an initial purchase price and then an annual subscription fee so that an organization can stay current with the latest software updates and have access to product support. These software purchase prices can range from $5,000 to $11,000, depending on the software type and manufacturer. The annual subscription costs can range from $695 to $1,345 per year, per license. See Figure 3.1 for a breakdown of the cost of software.

As software costs continue to rise, software manufacturers are reducing the time period during which they will provide support for older software versions, forcing firms to purchase new software more frequently than they would like in order to have their products supported. This, along with the rising demand for BIM services, will only exacerbate the situation.

As architects, engineers, and general contractors grapple with software costs and file storage issues, they must also deal with the network itself. To maximize new hardware and software capabilities, firms need to upgrade their infrastructure, including their local area network (LAN) and their wide area network (WAN), which may entail the use of WAN optimization systems such as Riverbed Technologies. In addition to the software and file storage issues, another issue that must be addressed by the IT department is an organization's Internet connection. Firms must have a fast Internet connection to ensure the ability to make large file transfers to/from their clients with minimal delays. The cost for faster Internet connections had been coming down in recent years but has since increased steadily over the past year. Unfortunately, all of these upgrades are not cheap. In fact, if an organization wants to do this correctly, it needs to understand it will cost a small fortune and will not be a one-time investment. These IT costs appear expensive without context to a firm's strategic plan. Many firms have a tactical view of IT

Software	Initial Cost	Annual Subscription
Revit Architecture	$6,000.00	$695.00
NavisManage	$11,000.00	$1,345.00
Solibri	$7,000.00	$1,000.00

Figure 3.1 Software costs.

and think of it as a necessary evil to operate the practice of architecture. IT leadership is emerging in firms where IT is viewed as a strategic advantage.

BIM is also affecting the legal department. Architects face many issues beyond that of the software and the technical IT costs. Architects need to know how the registered architect of record on a project will provide oversight on their project. They need to decide how the performance reviews of the project will be done and how the CDs will be delivered, including if they will be providing a model. If a model is provided, the architects need to decide if there are going to be any costs to the owner as well as what information will be allowed in the model. The architect of record needs to know what liability he or she will have when providing the model along with the construction drawings. In addition to the obstacles facing the deliverables to the owner, firms also have to consider how BIM will impact other parts of the business, such as human resources.

A big challenge facing firms is the BIM paradigm shift's impact on human resources. In my experience, during a paradigm shift many companies make things up as they go along, and this practice is permitted because everything is new. People are allowed to improvise as they go along because there is no standard to fall back on. The problem with everyone making things up is that it causes a lack of definition and consistency. This lack of definition and consistency has a major impact on human resources where job descriptions need to be locked in for a period of time in order for new resources to be interviewed and hired. An example would be the title of BIM coordinator. The problem is that currently the job description for a BIM coordinator is either nonexistent or varies wildly from organization to organization. In most firms, the project manager is going to want to know who is working on or billing to his or her job and what the capabilities of that person are and what can or cannot be expected of the person. A decision has to be made about whether that employee is going to add value to the project or if he or she is going to siphon away needed budget with no beneficial results. If an organization does decide to create new titles, then the titles need to have a clear definition regarding what that person can and cannot provide, while also proving that the person is the best fit for that job. Firms also need to look to the industry to make certain that their titles and jobs align with the rest of the industry.

A TALE FROM THE TRENCHES

When I was working in an engineering department and I required resources, I would notify the HR department of my needs. My organization was very detailed when it came to job duties and responsibilities. If I needed three engineering technicians—Level 3, Concrete Specialists—I would tell the resource manager of my needs, and she would make certain that I had the correct resources available. In other words, I knew what to expect when I made my request, and I knew that I would receive the resources that were needed. When I see "BIM coordinator" listed as a resource on my job, I do not feel as confident in their knowledge and abilities. I start asking questions pertaining to the experience that they have acquired, the school they attended, and the knowledge they have about the building. For verification, I would request their certifications and examples of past work. The fact that firms have to go to the extent of asking these questions shows that this is a huge problem. The only structured training is generally for learning the use of the software. This reminds me of when, back in 1994, I saw a job opening for a "Web designer with ten years of Web design experience."

Conversely, there are people who are very knowledgeable about BIM. These are the people who "eat, sleep, and dream" BIM. They are the ones who spend their off-hours blogging about BIM and likely have vanity license plates on their car that read "BIMMASTER." They are the true BIM experts, and these are the people who should really be kept on board. The problem is that their services are in high demand, and in many cases, their salary requirements begin to pose a problem. BIM is so important that, even in this difficult economy, BIM specialists are asking for higher salaries to stay on board—and they are getting them. Some small firms cannot afford their salaries and many large firms cannot justify the salaries, which puts those firms at a competitive disadvantage with BIM. Currently, every aspect of our industry is being touched by BIM, and thus the industry is truly experiencing a paradigm shift. Everything is changing—even the way design firms work with customers. The AEC industry is changing. For a better understanding, break out the functions of an organization into three areas: people, process, and platform. Now, look at how BIM is affecting these three areas. BIM is affecting people through modeling. Production staffs now model instead of drawing two-dimensional (2-D) lines and circles with no intelligence in CAD. Another change is that the modelers can see the building coming together as they model in ways they never could have in a 2-D environment. Modelers can also see how different systems fit together and gain a greater knowledge of the building than was ever possible with CAD or hand drafting. BIM is affecting the design process. To see how BIM has affected the platform, look at the network, servers, and workstations. If the industry were to do a survey, it would find that most firms doing BIM now tend to go out and buy the top-of-the-line servers, workstations, and laptops available because BIM software requires a lot of memory, processor speed, storage space, and video capability.

A TALE FROM THE TRENCHES

There is an organization in California that hired a vice president of virtual construction. The first question that comes to mind is, "What does 'virtual construction' mean?" In our industry, virtual construction refers to the ability to build a building in 3-D on a computer. To do virtual construction is more than just creating a massing model. It requires constructing the building in Revit, Bentley BIM, or any other software program exactly as the building will be built in the field. Once we understand what virtual construction is, the next question becomes whether or not this person really is a vice president. In most cases, the answer would be no. This person was a highly valued BIM resource who demanded more money than the organization's pay bands would allow. In order to bring this person on board, the organization had to create a vice president–level position so that it could pay him the salary that he required. This is what is happening at some large firms. In many of the smaller firms that can afford to pay higher salaries, there are BIM managers who are making as much as the partners. Again, these firms have to pay the really experienced BIM resources much more in order to keep them on or get them on their staff in the first place. As BIM continues to spread, this is where the pay scales are going because there is still a huge and ever-increasing demand for highly qualified BIM resources. BIM should not be a job in itself in most organizations but rather a capability. I don't recall, but I do not believe accounting firms built spreadsheet departments.

Due to the slow adoption of change in the AEC community, paradigm shifts such as BIM take place over longer periods of time. Because of the slow pace of change, the impact does not feel as game changing. Exploring other paradigm shifts can lend perspective to the BIM paradigm shift.

Historical Paradigm Shifts

Because BIM has led to a paradigm shift in the AEC community, a better understanding of the shift can be had by looking at some paradigm shifts from the past. One paradigm shift that has affected a large majority of people in the United States and throughout the world would be the shift from regular mail, also known as "snail mail," to e-mail. In this shift, there was an intervening step in the process, which was the fax. In the early part of the twentieth century, all written correspondence was sent either by regular mail or by telegram. Telegrams were used for short, urgent communications, and regular mail was used for all other forms of written communication. Regular mail was a slow process but was the only cheap and reliable way to get written correspondence delivered. As the century progressed, the use of telephones increased. As a result of the increase in telephone use, much of the written communication practices that were previously used became vocally communicated. Regular mail, however, was still used for sending official documents, postcards, and letters. With the advent of the fax machine in the 1950s, people began to send some of their documents (especially official documents) via fax, prior to sending the original documents via regular mail. This mode of communication helped to streamline some industries such as real estate. Sending a home offer letter through regular mail was a slow process. Now, with the fax machine, real estate agents could fax documents needed for closing rather than hand delivering them or sending them via regular mail. This also allowed banks to do business more easily in outlying areas as they could still get the information needed in a timely manner, even if they were hundreds or thousands of miles away.

In 1965, one of the first e-mail systems was set up at the Massachusetts Institute of Technology (MIT). This e-mail system was called Mailbox and was limited to people at MIT. E-mail has completely revolutionized the idea of mail and communication.

The only limitation has been access to the Internet. E-mail usage from 1965 to 1980 was limited to university computer networks and large company mainframes. The general public had no way to access the Internet until the 1990s. In 1990, Internet usage was less than 1 percent of the U.S. population. Today, this figure stands at 75.9 percent of the U.S. population.

This new system can provide instantaneous delivery of mail to recipients. As the technology has progressed, we find that now official documents, photos, and the like can also be sent via e-mail. E-mail has had such an impact on society that people now expect a response to their e-mails in minutes rather than in days or weeks. Today, over 600 million people worldwide use e-mail. In the United States, e-mail has become so common that the amount of regular mail delivered by the U.S. Postal Service (USPS) is beginning to decline. Figure 3.2 shows the actual first-class mail volume for the first three quarters of the last three years. Overall, first-class delivery has dropped by 5,191,003, or 10 percent, over the past three years, down from 26,346,053 pieces for the first three quarters of 2008 to 21,155,050 for the first three quarters of 2010.

Speed has become the driving force in this dramatic rise in the use of e-mail. Speed has also had an impact on another historical paradigm shift.

As I mentioned earlier, regular mail was used for written correspondence and official business. The telephone, invented in 1876 by Alexander Graham Bell, brought about another, slow-moving paradigm shift. The telephone did not become widely used until the 1920s. By the 1950s, over 80 percent of the population of the United States had a telephone or had access to a telephone. As AT&T's famous ad put it, "Reach out and touch someone." The telephone offered a means of contacting friends and family that had not been

First Class Pieces Handled by USPS					
Quarter	2010	% Change	2009	% Change	2008
1	8,141,613	(7.20%)	8,769,168	(10.30%)	9,773,164
2	6,555,367	(12.50%)	7,898,894	(11.20%)	8,451,281
3	6,456,060	(8.10%)	7,026,386	(13.50%)	8,119,600

Figure 3.2 USPS chart.

available before. This ability to communicate verbally with people across town or across the country or even the world soon became used by business, which gave rise to the conference call. Businesses found that some meetings could be conducted via conference call instead of in person. This saved companies a large amount of money on travel expenses and lost productivity while traveling.

The next big shift was from the conference call to the video conference call. One of the major negatives of the conference call had been that people could not see each other during the call. This inability to see each other meant that people couldn't read each other's body language. This meant that sales representatives tended to do more in-person meetings rather than conference calls as body language is very important in the sales transaction. With the use of video conference calls, this barrier was removed. Now businesses could save thousands of dollars a year by using videoconferencing rather than flying their employees to other cities for meetings. Videoconferencing is also being used for personal conversations via Skype, MSN Messenger, and Yahoo! Messenger, to mention a few. These advances have completely changed how we communicate with people and allow us to communicate locally as well as with people on the other side of the globe. These technologies have become very inexpensive and pervasive.

In reviewing historical paradigm shifts, we must also include the transition from telegrams to landline telephones to cell phones. As mentioned above, telegrams were used for urgent, short communications. The landline telephone provided a fundamental change in that people could actually talk to each other rather than sending written messages. This was a huge change and enabled people to stay in touch with each other more than they had in the past. The invention of the cell phone further changed this dynamic by providing people the opportunity to be "available" twenty-four hours a day, seven days a week. I will go into the cell phone paradigm shift in more depth later in this chapter.

Responding to a Paradigm Shift

The AEC community has been the first to respond to the BIM paradigm shift. The first step is to recognize that a paradigm shift has taken place. There are many architecture firms and general contractors out there that still have not acknowledged that a paradigm shift has taken place in our industry. These firms are continuing to use CAD to prepare their plans with no real thought about BIM. Many of these firms are resistant to BIM. They do not want to change the way that they do things, and they see BIM as a threat to the status quo.

Once an organization recognizes that a paradigm shift has occurred and acknowledges that it must adapt, the organization needs to assess what impact this change will have on its business and how it needs to respond. The important thing at this point is for firms not to panic. As long as the acknowledgment of the paradigm shift has occurred and the change is embraced, then plans can be made to adapt the organization's business model to the changed environment. The first step firms can take is to perform a SWOT analysis. A SWOT analysis is when an organization identifies its strengths, weaknesses, opportunities, and threats. The paradigm shift would definitely qualify as a threat in this case. The SWOT analysis will be explained in more depth later in this chapter.

The owner community lags behind the AEC community. Most owners do not have a framework for studying this paradigm shift. In response to the lack of a methodology, a simple methodology has been developed for owners to use, called the 4E methodology. While it has specific application to BIM, it can be easily adapted to any catalyst driving a paradigm shift. In fact, this methodology was spawned from previous consulting work in the telecommunications industry where the "dial tone" business leadership was struggling to understand why the "Internet" mattered and how it would affect their business. The four Es are

1. Educate
2. Evaluate
3. Experience
4. Execute

The benefit of the 4E methodology is that it applies to any owner, of any size, regardless of constraints. It is especially useful when an owner would like to "stick its toe in the water." Figure 3.3 sums up the 4E methodology in graphic form.

The *educate* phase is the most critical step. In lieu of biased vendor education, an owner must develop a structured method of

4E Methodology

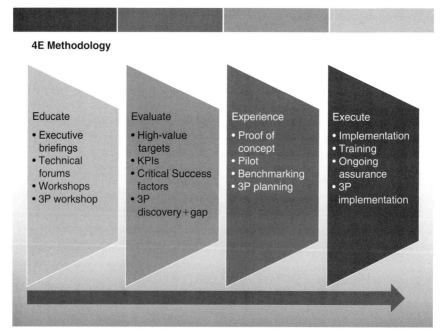

Educate	Evaluate	Experience	Execute
• Executive briefings	• High-value targets	• Proof of concept	• Implementation
• Technical forums	• KPIs	• Pilot	• Training
• Workshops	• Critical Success factors	• Benchmarking	• Ongoing assurance
• 3P workshop	• 3P discovery + gap	• 3P planning	• 3P implementation

Figure 3.3 Four Es.

understanding the opportunity. Most owners believe that BIM training involves the training of staff on the actual BIM application. (By the way, picking up this book is a great first step.) Developing a plan to educate an owner organization starts at the top and moves all the way down. This can be achieved through executive briefings, workshops, seminars, and white papers. There is a wealth of information available in the current marketplace. This information should always be assessed based on authorship and sponsorship. A white paper developed by a software company will have value, but it should be understood that the message will be biased because it was probably the brainchild of the marketing department. Any complimentary education is never complimentary and, however subtle, is a marketing tactic. Complimentary education is a great place to start, but, at some point, having unbiased paid education is a must. Hands-on software training would also be a good idea but is not a must. The goal is to have an understanding of how BIM could help an organization. The best idea of how BIM can help an owner will, in fact, come from the owner. This will only happen when owners understand how BIM can be used in their specific organization.

The true test as to whether sufficient effort was spent on the educate phase becomes clear during the *evaluate* phase. The evaluate phase starts by finding at least three high-value targets. A high-value target is a business problem that BIM could solve that will potentially drive the greatest near-term return. Without a good understanding of the capabilities and limitations of BIM, it might be difficult to identify these high-value targets. Once these high-value targets are identified, it is important to understand their associated key performance indicators (KPIs). Many high-value targets have a subjective value definition. An actual KPI with a method of measurement must be deployed. The development of a high-value target typically starts with a problem statement. For example: "BIM can help to improve the construction schedules." The KPI for this problem statement would be the difference (likely percentage) of planned completion versus actual completion. KPIs are analytical by definition and should be treated as such. The next criterion that requires development is the critical success factors. Developing critical success factors that are in alignment with the high-value targets is critical. A critical success factor is a condition that is tied to the overall organization's success. In the preceding example, assume that the organization is a retail group. Improved construction schedules would likely be tied to the critical success factor to gain market share. This would be accomplished by deploying retail outlets at a faster pace.

Once these three high-value targets have been evaluated, they must be prioritized for the next phase of experience.

These three high-value targets will be developed as proof of concepts (POCs). Based on these POCs, a BIM *execution* plan is developed to utilize BIM as a transformative technology to assist in solving the problem. The execution plan should be designed to directly affect the KPI in a positive direction. These projects are executed based on the plan, and the results are tracked and summarized. If the objective is to reduce requests for information (RFIs) on a given project, the number of RFIs would be the KPI. The BIM execution plan would be based on utilizing BIM for a constructability review. Based on identifying RFIs prior to construction, the project will have fewer RFIs during construction. There are cases where the POC does not have a direct positive outcome, but becomes a learning experience to be applied to the next POC. The feedback and results from the experience phase are then applied to the execute phase.

The *experience* phase allows for managing BIM in a controlled environment with focus on tangible gains in the enterprise. These lessons are designed into a BIM rollout program. The program would not likely be rolled out overnight and applied to every project. As an example, a large retailer may decide that it will first roll out its BIM initiative on all new construction in the Southeast. Then it may execute the BIM initiative to one region per year over a five-year period.

This method is effective in that an owner can spend a little, learn a lot, and then receive a return.

Organizational Impact of a Paradigm Shift

One big change that has occurred as part of the paradigm shift is that firms have gone from being generalists to being specialists. In the past, architects and engineers were all in one place. These multidisciplinary firms could do everything in-house. For the most part, they did not contract out or hire consultants. Over time, because of geography and technology, firms have become more specialized. If an architecture firm is working on a hospital and they are looking for a mechanical engineer, they need to decide if they are going to go with the closest, cheapest, most convenient mechanical engineer or if they are going to go with an organization that has a great deal of experience with health care and hospital projects. As long as the organization with the specialized experience is registered in the same referred state, the architecture firm can use that organization on its project. Our industry has progressed to the point that we will scour the country, sometimes even the world, to find the best firms that specialize in what we need. We will use these specialists instead of using the local organization that is more of a generalist organization. A good example of this is the waterproofing consulting industry. If a general contractor is working on a project in Dubai, do they hire the local organization here in the United States? Unless the local organization has expertise in the field and has the ability to work overseas, the answer would be no, they would go with an organization that has a great deal of experience. This has resulted in a great many of these waterproofing consultants flying all over the world. We also see this in fields outside of construction. For example, over the past six years, there has been much rapid growth and expansion in the Middle East, but it has moved so fast there that there are likely to be significant problems with construction. We will see that, over the next two years, there will be a large amount of litigation in Dubai because of these construction problems. We have already seen that major construction law firms have established offices in Dubai. Again, we will find the specialist law firms, not the generalists. In other words, an owner won't find an attorney in Dubai dealing with construction litigation that handles divorces and/or bankruptcies back in the United States. This is another prime example of how firms seek out the most experienced and not the most convenient companies. This trend toward specialists has also influenced the way that we work—pick the best organization for the job, period.

Cultural Assessment

The changes that have been brought about by technology in the twentieth century have moved us from being firms that are silos—working off by ourselves as self-contained entities that have expertise in as many fields as possible—to firms that are more collaborative. Thirty years ago, Heery was a good example of a silo company. It tried to do as much as possible in-house. Today, we find that our firms work more closely with other firms to draw on their expertise rather than trying to be the experts in everything. With the changes from silos to collaboration and from generalists to specialists, our method of networking has also undergone a dramatic change from in-person networking to online social networking using Facebook, LinkedIn, and other social media sites. These sites have provided us with the ability to connect to far more people than we were ever able to do in the past. A person may say that he or she has 400 friends on Facebook, but usually not all of these people are really his or her friends but are more along the lines of acquaintances. The efficiency of social networking tools may not exist, but the pace and ability to message requirements of capabilities is tremendous. These social media sites have also taken their place in our recruiting and human resources (HR) departments. Recruiters are using social networking sites to discover information about prospective candidates. We also see these sites being used by HR departments and sometimes direct supervisors. Managers like to keep up with what their employees are doing, and social media sites provide a quick and easy way to do this. Social media has become an effective way to find talent.

Companies have also provided employees with the ability to collaborate through enterprise resource planning (ERP) systems. These ERP systems are an integrated and sometimes Internet-based system used to manage internal and external resources. The purpose of an ERP is to facilitate the flow of information between all business functions (collaboration). Although many of these ERP systems are Internet based, some firms decide to host the system on their own network. As we move from silos to collaboration, our corporate culture also changes. In the past, if we needed information from the accounting department, we would have to physically visit or call or even send a memo requesting information. With online or hosted ERP systems, we do not have to physically go to the accounting department as there are now portals built into the ERP where we can access the needed information online. All of these advancements lead us to wonder if technology is driving culture or if culture is driving technology.

In many areas, technology has outstripped our ability to adapt, leaving us trying to "catch up." We see this often in the medical field, where new miracle drugs can extend someone's life but do not necessarily improve the quality of that life. This leaves people fighting over whether or not to use the drugs. Unfortunately, our legal system cannot keep up with these advancements, and these questions end up in long, drawn-out legal battles. Another example of technology driving culture would be MP3 players. Traditionally, people were limited to the radio stations that broadcast in their local markets, and they listened either to music or talk radio. Now, with MP3 players, people can download what they want to listen to and never even turn on their car radio. This is having a huge impact on local radio stations, which have seen their listenership drop dramatically over the past few years. The ability to buy single songs and store them on an MP3 device has also had a huge impact on the recording industry, which is still trying to adjust to this paradigm shift. With MP3s, consumers end up having a much more narrow experience than they did when they listened to the radio. Now they can tune out all other opinions and types of music that they do not like. This leads us to wonder about the person who has 400 friends on Facebook. We must ask, Is this person so extroverted that he or she can make friends with this many people or is the person so introverted that he or she has to use Facebook as a platform to make friends. If the latter is true, then technology is definitely driving culture.

The Velocity of Technology Adoption

Since the 1990s, the term "paradigm shift" has come to represent the changes to our lifestyles brought on by advancements in technology. Another way to look at this would be a case of "reality versus actuality" or "technology driving culture instead of culture driving technology." A good representation of this change outside of the industry (but at the same time affecting all industries) would be the invention and use of the cellular or "cell" phone. In the United States, the landline telephone had been used since the late nineteenth century and had become the primary form of voice communication. Of course, landline telephones themselves had taken the place of telegrams in the late 1800s and were in more than 95 percent of U.S. households by the late 1960s. From the late 1920s, scientists had been working to create a cell or "mobile" telephone. These efforts went mostly unnoticed during the 1920s through the 1940s, as our culture had been adapting to the change from the telegram to the landline phone. During this same time period, mobile phone research progressed, culminating in the first cell phone call made on a handheld mobile phone in April of 1973. The problem with these first mobile phones was that the technology was not mature enough to make them commercially viable. If a person was over the age of twelve in the 1970s, he or she probably remembers seeing someone with the infamous "bag phone." These first mobile phones were very heavy and very expensive. Only the wealthy could afford these phones, and once they purchased one, they were faced with the problem of who to call. In the mid- to late 1970s, if a cell phone owner were out on a Saturday night and wanted to call someone, the person he or she was calling was most likely either out and had no mobile phone or was at home and would use a landline phone. The first cell or mobile phones did not catch on because of their size/weight, cost, and poor reception. The early phones attracted what Geoffrey Moore refers to in his book *Crossing the Chasm* as the "innovators." These innovators tend to be on the cutting edge of any technology. They want to try the next "new" thing regardless of the cost and regardless whether it works as advertised. To understand exactly where the innovators fit, we need to understand each of the five elements of Geoffrey Moore's technology adoption life cycle:

1. Innovators
2. Early adopters
—The chasm—

3. Early majority

4. Late majority

5. Laggards

The failure of the early cell phones to catch on did not mean that research and development stopped. The cell phone entered what Geoffrey Moore calls "the chasm." The chasm occurs when a new product is launched and then is removed or drastically rolled back from the market because of poor adoption. These products are then reworked and improved so that they can be relaunched at a later date. The problem is that the initial product was adopted by innovators and early adopters who liked to use it because it was new technology. When the cell phone companies tried to get pragmatists to adopt the cell phone, that's when it fell into the chasm. Cell phones fully emerged from the chasm in the mid- to late 1980s, when technology finally caught up with the concept of a cell phone. During the mid- to late 1980s, the country saw subscriber numbers increase by over 50 percent each year until 1991, when the total number of subscribers topped 7.5 million. By the late 1990s, new cell phone subscribers were increasing by only 25 to 27 percent per year. Although the first cell phone call was made in 1973, cell phone subscribers in the United States did not top 1 million until 1987 and did not break the 100 million mark until 2000. See Figure 3.4 for cell phone subscriber numbers in the United States from 1985 through 2008.

Another good example of the chasm stage would be the touch-based cell phone. Personal digital assistant (PDA)–like phones came out in the early 1990s. They were bulky and did not work very well. Because they did not work very well, these phones never made it past the early adopters and thus they went into the chasm and did not reemerge until the introduction of the iPhone in the early 2000s. The iPhone, although heavily marketed, still only makes up around 4 percent of the total U.S. cell phone market. If we look at the market share within the smart phone market, the iPhone controls 60 percent of the market as of June 2010. When a product emerges from the chasm, it moves to what Geoffrey Moore refers to as the "early majority" stage.

Now that we have a better understanding of the technology adoption life cycle, we need to look at and decide if BIM is heading toward or away from the chasm. This is a very good question as we are seeing some midsize architecture firms reduce the number

Year	Subscribers	Percent Change		Year	Subscribers	Percent Change
1985	340,213			1997	55,312,293	25.59%
1986	681,825	100.41%		1998	69,209,321	25.12%
1987	1,230,855	80.52%		1999	86,047,003	24.33%
1988	2,069,441	68.13%		2000	109,478,031	27.23%
1989	3,508,944	69.56%		2001	128,374,512	17.26%
1990	5,283,055	50.56%		2002	140,766,842	9.65%
1991	7,557,148	43.05%		2003	158,721,981	12.76%
1992	11,032,753	45.99%		2004	182,140,362	14.75%
1993	16,009,461	45.11%		2005	207,896,198	14.14%
1994	24,134,421	50.75%		2006	233,000,000	12.08%
1995	33,758,661	39.88%		2008	262,700,000	12.75%
1996	44,042,992	30.46%				

Figure 3.4 Cell phone users.

of Revit licenses that they own rather than purchasing more. One organization in particular had 200 licenses of Revit but chose only to renew 50 licenses. Some would say that this is an indication that we are heading toward the chasm rather than away from it. Others are saying that this is related more to the economy's impact on firms rather than technology adoption. The organization mentioned above indicated that it had to lay off employees as a result of the downturn in the economy. The organization had a policy of "last in, first out," which resulted in a very large number of its BIM-proficient employees being laid off. Once this occurred, the organization was left with a more CAD-proficient work force, so in order to get projects done on time, the organization had to drop about 150 licenses of Revit and convert them to AutoCAD. For this organization, the reduction in the usage of BIM is directly related to the bad economy. In talking with the CEO of this organization, he has indicated that when the economy improves, the organization will definitely rehire its BIM staff and ramp up its usage of Revit. My advice was for him to use this as an opportunity to engage his more experienced staff with BIM.

Firms now need to figure out where they are on the technology adoption curve and make the necessary changes to stay up-to-date. This is very important because if the organization is going to drive any kind of BIM initiative, its needs to understand where it sits. For example, if the organization is a laggard and, after being asked to develop a BIM strategy, a manager goes to his boss with a $5 million BIM implementation budget, he could be jeopardizing his career. If the organization is an innovator or an early adopter, then that manager will have more leeway in her budget and ROI. An organization can have different strategies around BIM. An organization has to take small "baby steps" to implement BIM. Companies have to make the transition more slowly to get better returns rather than taking much larger steps.

In 2010, we traveled the country and held over thirty BIM executive briefings. The attendees ranged anywhere from 20 to 100 people per location. In these sessions, we conducted a brief survey based on Moore's adoption life cycle:

1. Where do you see yourself on the curve?
2. Where do you see your organization on the curve?
3. Where do you perceive your peers in this room are on the curve?

Interestingly enough, almost all of the attendees rated themselves as much earlier adopters than their organization. They believed that they were technology leaders in the organization. The majority of these technology leaders were not in leadership positions in their organization. The majority of firms believed that the other firms in the room were ahead of them in technology adoption.

Another interesting survey asked attendees to rate themselves on a scale of 1 to 10, 10 being an expert and 1 being that they had just heard about BIM. The majority rated themselves as 7 or greater (some rated themselves as a 20).

The reality is that BIM is not being adopted on an enterprise scale in the AEC community. Thus, the pain of a paradigm shift is not being felt at an enterprise level but rather at a localized level. This will continue to change and become prevalent at the enterprise level. Owner adoption and drive will continue to be the catalyst for

BIM. However, very few owners are driving BIM at an enterprise level within their own organization.

As we have seen with the paradigm shift, many firms experience the issue of "here is what I have, and now I need to start all over." The problem is that the large majority of firms cannot just shut down for a year and develop new procedures and processes to integrate BIM into their business. There are some very small firms that have the ability to shut down for six months in order to develop a great system to integrate BIM into their organization. As a part of this, they completely change the way they deliver and interact with their customers. They now do collaborative design with the owners and present 3-D renderings instead of flat 2-D renderings, but most companies do not have this opportunity. Adopting the technology is easy; adapting the business is the challenge. We have to make these changes within our current company framework while still delivering on current projects. This requires strategic planning. The first thing we have to do is perform a SWOT analysis, which involves identifying our strengths, weaknesses, opportunities, and threats. This is a core piece of strategic planning. When an organization carries out a SWOT analysis, it should always look at it from two perspectives: the organization's view and the manager's view. When we look at a paradigm shift, it is as much about what the company is going to do as it is about what the manager's career is going to look like in five years. One might say that the key to strategic planning is not to have a stash of huge three-ring binders that are never going to be used. Keep things short and simple.

The book *Good to Great: Why Some Companies Make the Leap . . . and Others Don't* by Jim Collins is one of my reading essentials and, for anyone who has attended my executive briefings, is one of my participation prizes. In this book, Collins introduces the hedgehog concept, which essentially states that simplicity is best. Collins addresses some key aspects of technology.

- Good-to-great organizations think differently about technology and technological change than mediocre ones.
- Good-to-great organizations avoid technology fads and bandwagons, yet they become pioneers in the application of carefully selected technologies.
- The key question about any technology is, "Does the technology fit directly with your Hedgehog Concept?" If yes,

than you need to become a pioneer in the application of that technology. If no, then you can settle for parity or ignore it entirely.

■ The good-to-great companies used technology as an accelerator of momentum, not a creator of it. None of the good-to-great companies began their transformations with pioneering technology, yet they all became pioneers in the application of technology once they grasped how it fit with their three circles and after they hit breakthrough.

■ You could have taken the exact same leading-edge technologies pioneered at the good-to-great companies and handed them to their direct competitors for free, and the competitors still would have failed to produce anywhere near the same results.

■ How a company reacts to technological change is a good indicator of its inner drive for greatness versus mediocrity. Great companies respond with thoughtfulness and creativity, driven by a compulsion to turn unrealized potential into results; mediocre companies react and lurch about, motivated by fear of being left behind.[2]

chapter

4

Strategic Planning

Strategic planning is the process by which an organization determines its direction and makes decisions to determine resource allocation to drive the organization in this direction. In a paradigm shift, having a strategic plan is critical. Most organizations undergo an annual strategic planning process. The level of seriousness around developing and implementing the strategic plan differs from organization to organization. While strategic planning is considered to be developing a long view of the organization, it can also be applied on a project basis as well. Depending on the organization, this could range from a one-year plan to a five-year plan. BIM implementation requires a strategic plan to be successful. When BIM is treated like a tactical tool, the outcomes are rarely successful and sometimes disastrous.

In my experience, there are only two stages that are critical to the success of a business. These stages are clarity and intensity. A great strategic plan should provide clarity to all stakeholders. Once a high level of clarity is reached, it can then be followed with tremendous intensity in execution. Intensity in execution allows an organization to allocate resources and meet objectives. It also gives the organization an opportunity to add additional resources to meet these objectives earlier if required. Many organizations do not reach the clarity stage. They then intensely allocate resources and still do not meet objectives.

A TALE FROM THE TRENCHES

The CEO of a large construction company attends a national construction conference. After seeing a few presentations on BIM and hearing from his peers about their investments in BIM, he returns to the home office. In a staff meeting, he asks his team about their understanding of BIM and goes on to explain that their competition is heavily into BIM and that they are behind. The information technology (IT) department is then tasked with implementing BIM in the company. The IT department proceeds tactically to evaluate the software available and purchases software and new hardware. They then proceed to attend days of training and develop proficiency in BIM. Success has been reported back to management. Business development now understands that the organization has BIM capability. A project is sold with BIM services included; it is budgeted based on the IT department's understanding of the scope. The team executes the work and it costs three times as much as budgeted and becomes irrelevant to the project delivery team. Deliverables are not usable to the project team and it becomes a marketing exercise. Since then, the organization has taken a step back and developed a strategic plan.

The dissipation of this work effort requiring additional resources just to meet the objectives is due to a lack of clarity.

There are many methodologies for developing a strategic plan. The methodology that I have used most frequently is developing a SWOT (strengths, weaknesses, opportunities, and threats) analysis. While SWOT is not a strategic plan in its entirety, it is a great methodology that can easily be deployed. It is also easily deployed on an enterprise level as well as at an individual construction project level.

Development of a SWOT Analysis for an Owner

SWOT analysis is a strategic planning method used to evaluate the strengths, weaknesses, opportunities, and threats involved in a project or business (see Figure 4.1).

Strengths: These are attributes of the organization that will be helpful in achieving the desired results.

Weaknesses: These are attributes of the organization that will be harmful in achieving the desired results.

Action (Build/Buy/Partner)	Strengths	Weaknesses
	1.People 2.Process 3.Platform	1.People 2.Process 3.Platform
Opportunities	*How do I use my strengths to take advantage of the opportunities?*	*How do I overcome my weaknesses that keep me from taking advantage of the opportunities?*
	1.People 2.Process 3.Platform	1.People 2.Process 3.Platform
Threats	*How do I use my strengths to mitigate threats?*	*How do I overcome my weaknesses that will make these threats a reality?*

Figure 4.1 SWOT analysis chart.

Opportunities: These are external conditions that are helpful in achieving the desired results.

Threats: These are external conditions that could be harmful in achieving the desired results.

In a SWOT analysis, an organization basically maps out its strengths, weaknesses, opportunities, and threats. When the organization maps out its strengths versus opportunities, how can it use its strengths to take full advantage of the opportunities ahead, and what are the strengths of the implementation manager and the organization? To perform a true SWOT analysis, a company needs to look past the obvious strengths of experience and resources. The organization needs to look at all aspects of its business to identify its strengths and weaknesses.

These strengths and weaknesses should not only be limited to outward-facing capabilities. Following are some typical functional areas in a business:

- Sales—new business
- Sales—account management
- Marketing
- Business development

- Strategic alliances
- Operational excellence
- Specialized technical competence
- Company culture
- Human resources—career development
- Project management
- Project accounting
- Financial controls and policy
- Process management and documentation
- Technology innovation
- Information technology systems
- Industry leadership

A TALE FROM THE TRENCHES

To this end, most organizations would never consider accounting to be one of their strengths. Having worked at a large engineering organization, I saw that accounting was one of our company's strengths. This organization took accounting very seriously and turned it from just being a general and administrative (G&A) expense to being a true asset. A good example of how well the accounting department worked would be the accounts receivable (AR) department. AR was not something that I particularly enjoyed doing, so it wasn't at the top of my "to-do" list. When I had invoices that were over thirty days old, the accounting person responsible for my accounts would pressure me to get the invoices collected. She would call me and e-mail me and if she did not hear back from me, she would even go to the extreme of watching the parking lot to see when I arrived so that she could meet me and give me an aging report showing all of my invoices that were overdue as well as copies of the invoices themselves. She would not leave me alone until I told her what I was going to do to take care of each of the outstanding invoices. She would then follow up with me until all of the invoices were paid. This often involved numerous "parking lot" meetings. To the company's credit, she was not the only person in accounting doing this. All of the other people in AR were just as tenacious as she was. It was a part of their accounting culture. This engineering organization was also good at expense reporting. We all know that people do not like doing expense reports and that many companies are traditionally bad at actually communicating how to fill out an expense report correctly. My organization took what was usually a weakness for other firms and turned it into a strength. This was possible because they were very good at communicating how to fill out the expense reports and when to submit them. This accounting strength is not something that the marketing department developed, but it did help this organization get large federal contract work as well as work. The accounting disciplines positioned them to easily meet compliance requirements without increasing their overhead. Many firms shy away from federal work due to these overhead increases. Strong accounting systems are a must to win government work as they integrate well with the processes and procedures of government projects. Remember that an organization has to look at all aspects of their company to identify strengths and weaknesses. Not all of an organization's strengths are going to be on the company Web site and marketing material.

An owner's strength could be the ability to control the operating costs of a building through strong facility management (FM) systems.

Next, a company needs to identify its weaknesses. It will go about this in the same way that it identified its strengths, by looking at all aspects of its business. One of the first areas to look at would be the IT infrastructure. It is a common thread throughout most industries that no one believes that IT does a great job. People always feel that the IT department is behind the times and cannot keep up. The shortcomings of an organization's IT department can be seen by clients as a weakness. Some firms look at their basic infrastructure as a weakness, while others feel confident about their infrastructure but feel that their IT resources are the weakness.

One threat that is facing many architects, general contractors, engineers, and owners is whether to move from AutoCAD to BIM. In this case, these firms have to decide whether they want to outsource BIM or whether they want to buy software. If they decide to buy software, they will also have to determine what product to purchase. Currently, there are three primary software applications being used for BIM. These are Revit by Autodesk, Bentley BIM(Microstation) by Bentley, and ArchiCAD by Graphisoft. The latest market share data that we have is from 2007 (see Figure 4.2).

In Figure 4.2, the Bentley 2-D and 3-D products are tabulated together for a total of 11 percent of the market share. Graphisoft's ArchiCAD is in the "Other" category. The AutoCAD numbers include 2-D and 3-D. In 2007, Architectural Desktop, an AutoCAD program, was still being pushed heavily by Autodesk, which would account for the high percentage for AutoCAD in this chart. Since that time, however, Autodesk has focused more on its Revit products and less on Architectural Desktop. Our nonscientific surveys of our clients show

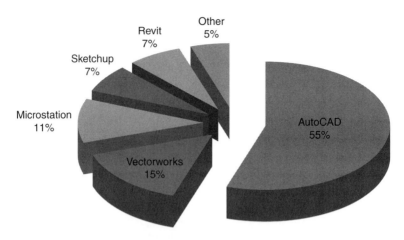

Figure 4.2 AEC market share, 2007
Source: Garner Research.

that the majority of them are using Revit followed by Bentley BIM. Any new study would need to break out the 2-D and 3-D products to gain a better knowledge of true BIM usage. It would be expected that new research similar to that on which this chart is based would reflect a rise in the use of Revit and Bentley BIM.

Once an organization understands what software to purchase, it needs to perform an investment assessment. In every other industry, when an organization buys software, there is a rule of thumb on how much it will spend on consulting services. This number is typically five to ten times what is spent on the actual software. The biggest challenge that we see is determining how much to spend on training, consulting, and integration for BIM. Unfortunately, in our industry, we typically do the opposite of what other industries do with software. We spend about a third of what we spent on the software for training, consulting, and integration. We buy the tool, but we never really train on it or implement it well. In most cases, the attitude is that we have very smart people and there is Web-based training available, so we'll just have them do that training and that will be adequate. Many firms in the architecture, engineering, and construction (AEC) industry approach new software in this way and then are surprised at the bad outcomes. The key point here is that the organization should develop a training and implementation plan and strategy prior to buying any licenses. Once the company has developed a plan, it will realize that if funds are limited, it will be better to purchase fewer licenses and focus more on training.

A TALE FROM THE TRENCHES

I did some consulting for a large subcontractor where we executed a BIM executive session for their executives to discuss BIM and their vision for becoming enabled with BIM, organization planning to determine changes and restructuring within their entire organization, and the technology implications for their culture. Days after the session, the CEO contacted me and said that his top two estimators, who had been with the organization forever, came to him and said that if the organization implemented this BIM strategy, they would quit; they would not be replaced by technology. My response was, "What are you going to do when they quit?" I told the CEO that this was the time for him to show leadership and drive the business in the direction of his vision. He could not allow his organization's future to be dictated by two people. This is something that will happen in many different firms and management needs to be aware of it and be ready to deal with it prior to starting any BIM implementation. Dealing with this sort of issue should be included in the BIM implementation plan and strategy.

The other thing that typically happens is that we say, "Let's go figure this thing out and get it set up because we have a project coming online and we are going to learn on that project." This strategy is rarely successful. The problem is that, as an industry, we would never say, "Let's take a project from last year and create a test bed and figure it out first before we go live with it." We rarely try to do any sort of benchmarking of our projects. We find that planning and strategy is the difference between "ready, aim, fire" and "fire, aim, ready." Unfortunately, everyone tends to underestimate what it takes. From the CEO to the modeler, we all feel we can do BIM with little formal training. What we should be doing is taking the small steps: do not try to get ten licenses; get one and purchase the correct level of training. Owners find themselves in the worst possible situation with BIM, because they typically have to start from scratch with BIM or outsource/partner with another organization. As we move forward, the next step is to perform a risk assessment.

When an organization plans ahead and is very narrow in its focus, it can actually perform a return-on-investment (ROI) assessment. For every dollar that is spent, the organization should expect to have a projected return. This assessment may be that for every dollar that is spent, the organization expects no return, but intends to break even. The point is that there should be an expectation of return. An organization cannot just spend money and not have any idea of the return that it will get. That type of behavior can lead to dire consequences. We, as an industry, need to remember that if we spend money on something, we should get something in return. That's just good business. For example, a major airline such as Delta or United would not buy planes not knowing what return they would be receiving on them, but instead they would have calculated what return they expect for the life of the plane. As owners begin to implement BIM, they must look at the return they will receive from it. Owners need to determine how BIM can provide ROI throughout the building life cycle.

The problem is that when organizations try to "boil the ocean," or do everything at once, they tend to buy software licenses without a plan, and they tend to struggle through the implementation. A year later, they may look back and think that BIM cost them more than it was worth. This exact scenario has played out at countless firms. These firms had no plan and no expectation of return, and when they failed, they blamed it on BIM, not on their lack of planning. If a company doesn't have a good plan and if it doesn't have an expectation of return, then that year's worth of effort is all very subjective; it is not analytical at all. If there is a good plan in place and management has an expectation of return, then the organization should be able to see which established benchmarks were met and whether or not it broke even on BIM. These companies would also be able to see that they will not get early returns from BIM. They should expect to attain a return in three years, and it should be 2 to 2.5 times what they spent on BIM implementation. What we have to remember is that planning for the ROI is very hard to do, and what we do as architects, engineers, general contractors, and owners is very complicated. We have people and projects, and our project teams are extended beyond our control. Tracking all of this becomes extremely hard when an organization tries to do everything at once. If an organization has a narrow focus, then it can more easily focus on what those returns are and manage them well.

Next, an organization needs to determine how to handle threats. See Figure 4.1 for the SWOT analysis chart. On this chart, the most difficult quadrant is the weaknesses and threats. "Risks are things that can happen without having any deliberate intention to cause harm behind them. A threat is something that is done by a competitor or

A TALE FROM THE TRENCHES

I worked on several projects with an architectural organization that had numerous IT issues. This organization of sixty-plus employees had a three-person IT department and was preparing to implement BIM because it felt it would fall behind the competition if it did not use BIM. The problem was that the organization saw its IT department as a weakness instead of a strength. It viewed the IT department as a weakness because the IT department could barely support the company using AutoCAD. The IT department also had problems with basic computer mainte-nance in that it took them several days to diagnose and fix a problem. These types of issues can cause huge production headaches for any organization when there is a resource without a computer to work with and work piling up ahead of a deadline.

This organization's answer to its IT weakness was to fire the entire IT department, all three of them. Management felt that since the IT department was already hav-ing problems keeping up, it would never be able to support the company once Revit was rolled out. Before actually firing the IT department, management had to make a decision as to what they were going to do to replace their IT department. As they examined their options, they realized that they could partner with another organization or they could contract services from an IT outsourcing company. This architectural organization decided to partner with a mechanical contractor that had a great IT department. The two firms had been working together for about twenty years prior to this problem and the architectural organization had been very impressed with the mechanical contractor's IT department. The mechanical organization had already been through implementing Revit.

adversary to offset whatever you have done."[1] How does an organi-zation overcome weaknesses to make sure that threats do not become a reality? Firms need to have a plan for how to deal with risks and threats. This is the scary part of the SWOT analysis, as the organiza-tion has to figure out what to do. Firms must understand that not doing anything is not an option.

The Three Ps

The three Ps refer to people, process, and platform. *People* are con-sidered the employees of an organization or the members of a project team. A first step is for firms to understand that one of the greatest assets that they have is their people. In order for an organization to take advantage of its assets, it must first understand them. Owners, architects, and engineering firms need to understand not only the strengths and weaknesses of their people but also their wants and needs. A happy and motivated employee will do a much better job than a disgruntled employee. Companies will also find that if people enjoy what they do, then they could become dedicated, lifelong employees. A good example of this is an organization that I did consulting work for. It has really dedicated people who have been with the company for twenty-five, thirty, even thirty-five years. These people enjoy their jobs and are very dedicated to the company. Some people would view this as a weakness because they feel that long-time employees are more resistant to change. I do not consider this a weakness; in fact, I consider this to be a strength, as it provides continuity and stability. The institutional knowledge that a long-term employee possesses is of great value; the challenge for management is to keep the employee motivated to leverage this knowledge for the benefit of the organization.

Change will drive a common discomfort to staff in an organization. In Bryson/Yetmes' book, *The Owner's Dilemma*, they have developed a great guideline for creating guiding principles that will assist in alleviating this discomfort. "A list of values and guiding principles should be simple, clear and easily communicated. My list includes the following:

Strive for transparency because information is power.
  ▪ Tell the truth . . . always.
Lead with exuberance and caring consideration.
  ▪ Manage clearly, consistently and cooperatively.
  ▪ Create a safe, it's-OK-to-screw-up environment.
  ▪ Attack processes, not people.
  ▪ Balance risk and reward.
  ▪ Take responsibility: Put the target on your own forehead.
Seek excellence.
  ▪ It's not just about the building.
  ▪ Plan for excellence.

Make decisions at the most powerful (efficient) level and the most powerful moment.

  ▪ Encourage a culture of curiosity and knowledge.
  ▪ Collaboration means *everyone*.

Be tough when it is important to the team's success.

  ▪ Defend the pack.
  ▪ Have difficult discussions early.
  ▪ Don't go to bed mad.

Build and preserve relationships.

  ▪ Your mom was right—thank-you notes are important.
  ▪ Share a compliment. What does it cost?
  ▪ Celebrate milestones.

Give people what they need to do their jobs.

  ▪ Every discussion should end with the question, *What do you need from me?*
  ▪ We don't need a hero."[2]

Process includes the steps an organization needs to take to complete tasks and projects. There is a process for everything. One example of a process would be how an organization handles inbound sales phone calls. These calls are usually routed to an individual who takes down the information. This person most likely will enter the caller's information into an online or hosted sales management system, also known as an enterprise resource planning (ERP) system, to create a lead. ERP is a system that integrates areas such as planning, purchasing, sales, marketing, finance, and human resources.[3] The lead that has been created in the ERP is then forwarded to the proper salesperson for him or her to follow up on. When the salesperson contacts the lead, he or she then updates the information in the sales management system. If the person is interested in buying something, then the lead is converted into an opportunity, and the sale is noted in the sales management system. Although this is a quick example of a process, it shows that there are definite steps involved in taking an inbound sales call. The key to being successful in a business is creating a process for everything that is done. For a general contractor doing trade coordination, it is very important to have a set process that is followed on every project. If there is no process or plan in place, then the trade coordination effort can and most likely will be unsuccessful. Firms need to look at themselves and determine if they have good processes in place. Owners need to look at the process of delivery of a new building and determine what could be done better. Remember that processes are extremely important to the success or failure of an organization and of a project.

Platform, in most cases, refers to the network infrastructure, desktops, and laptops. Included here would be the Internet connection and any Internet-based project management, ERP, or sales management systems. If a company's platform is not stable, this will hurt its chances of being successful. One of the firms I worked with in the past provides a great example of this. This organization had really good people and great processes, but its platform was subpar. The organization did not want to spend the capital to upgrade its servers to address the space, speed, and memory requirements of the organization and felt that all it needed was to have a desktop computer with some extra memory and a larger disk drive as the server. Because of its unwillingness to invest the money required to upgrade the server, the organization jeopardized the entire business. One night while the tape backup was being performed, the desktop workstation serving as the server failed. It was a fatal error on the hard drive, and the data could not be recovered. The only thing that saved the organization was that earlier backups had been created. Unfortunately for this organization, the most current backup was three days old. In other words, all of the work that had been done over the past three days was lost. The organization ended up having to pay to have the work done twice and also had to spend the money to upgrade the server as well as paying to attempt to recover data from the old server's hard drive. This turned out to be a very costly decision for the organization. Companies need to understand that having the correct platform in place is critical to project success and to success as a whole. An unfortunate event like this highlights the dependency on technology. Investments in platform planning and execution are critical. This dependency is driving many owners to realize that their vendors' platform is an extension of their platform. This is not only important from a security perspective but also from a performance perspective. For owners, this is especially true for facility management systems.

Although these are three separate areas, firms will find that they are interrelated to the point that if the organization fails in one area, the overall project or company will be in danger of failure. It is important to take the time to hire good people, establish good processes, and invest in a strong platform so that firms can be successful in their projects and in their business as a whole.

Plan of Action

To move an organization forward, there are only three possible actions. An organization has the choice of build (in-house), buy an organization that already has executed change, or partner (strategic alliance). While a pragmatic approach should be taken to develop a plan of action, the highest degree of failure is not to act at all.

> When selecting a business strategy, it is important to remember that strategic alliances are just one business tool that, if used at the wrong time, can materially hurt an organization. You must be able to step back and analyze your three options: You should build a capacity in-house, yourself, buy it through an acquisition, or strategically partner. You don't have to choose one option. The real power and benefit to your organization often comes when you understand how all three of these strategic options can be used simultaneously in order to help your company address a new market opportunity.[4]
>
> Alliances do not make sense when an organization has the requisite skills and resources necessary to "win a battle" on its own in a targeted market space. Alliances do not make sense when you need to control a certain technology, skill, or capability to ensure your company's long-term success and profitability. If you have the capability or the market window won't stay open, if there are reasonably priced targets, and if you have the capital, then an acquisition can be a far better answer than an alliance. It is critical that your organization consider the appropriate trade-offs among these three options early in the strategy-setting process, and then execute on them when you've made your decisions.[5]

Chapter Summary Key Points

- SWOT analysis is a strategic planning method used to evaluate the strengths, weaknesses, opportunities, and threats involved in a project or business.

- The strengths are the attributes of the organization that will be helpful in achieving the desired results.
- The weaknesses are the attributes of the organization that will be harmful in achieving the desired results.
- The opportunities are external conditions that are helpful in achieving the desired results.
- The threats are the external conditions that could be harmful in achieving the desired results.
- To perform a true SWOT analysis, a company needs to look past the obvious strengths of experience and resources.
- Currently, three primary software applications are being used for BIM: Autodesk Revit, Bentley BIM (Microstation), and Graphisoft's ArchiCAD.
- An organization should develop a training and implementation plan and strategy prior to purchasing software.
- For every dollar spent, an organization should expect a return.
- The three Ps—people, process, and platform—are critical to effective strategic planning.
- People are considered the employees of an organization or the members of a project team.
- The process is the steps an organization takes to complete tasks and projects.
- The platform, in most cases, is the network infrastructure, desktops, and laptops.
- When selecting a business strategy, it is important to remember that strategic alliances are just one business tool that, if used at the wrong time, can materially hurt an organization.

chapter

5

Tactics

Gap Analysis

When organizations develop a plan, there should be a common knowledge of where they are with regard to people, processes, and platforms. These firms should also have a general idea of where they want to be. Unfortunately, a company cannot just "flip a switch" to move from one place to the other. Organizations must map out a plan of how to get from their current state to their desired state. As part of this process, firms must also take into account that "all is impacted—the nuts and bolts, the daily rituals of process, and the way we typically do things. All has to be deconstructed and then reconstructed; and it has to be done on the fly while operations are going on because systems cannot be shut down."[sic][1] This is a very important part of gap analysis and the subsequent plans for change.

Firms must take their overall plan and map it out step by step. This allows organizations to get the small wins on their way to the overall goal. This has a positive influence on individuals as well as the entire organization, because if either individuals or the organization had to wait until the end of the process to get any satisfaction, they would be waiting an extended period of time and would feel that no progress was taking place. It is critical for the overall success of the project that the organization have intermediate goals or accomplishments throughout the change process. As Roger Chevalier discussed in his article "GAP Analysis Revisited," "a reasonable goal, set in measures that the people must do the work can control, can also serve to motivate them toward closing the performance gap."[2]

The images in Figures 5.1 and 5.2 depict a gap analysis. The first thing an owner must do is determine the as-is condition. The as-is condition of a general contractor doing trade coordination, for

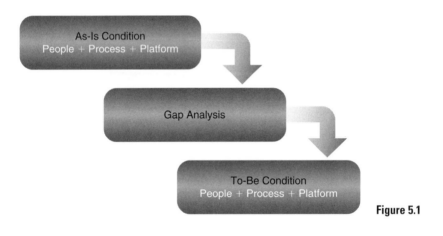

Figure 5.1

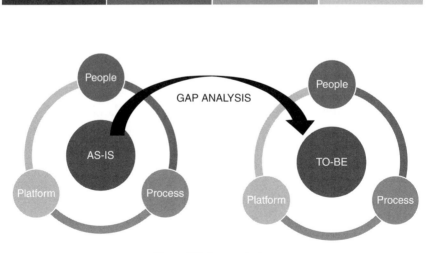

Figure 5.2 Gap analysis.

example, might be that it has a computer-aided design (CAD) department or, in some cases, a couple of drafters who will support the construction manager. The construction manager will get the plans and specs from the architect and then have the subcontractors (electrical, mechanical, plumbing, etc.) start the work from the two-dimensional (2-D) plans (as shown in Figure 5.3). The general contractor schedules trade coordination meetings, where 2-D plans are submitted and "coordinated" with the architectural and structural plans. The term "coordinated" is used because there is only so much that can be done in a 2-D environment. The plans are reviewed at the coordination meeting, and, following the reviews, the different subcontractors go back and make the changes so that they can resubmit their plans for the next coordination meeting. This continues until coordination is complete. This form of coordination resolves many problems, although there are still other issues that are left to be resolved in the field after construction has started. If this general contractor wants to move to BIM trade coordination, the first step after determining the as-is condition will be to decide on a to-be condition.

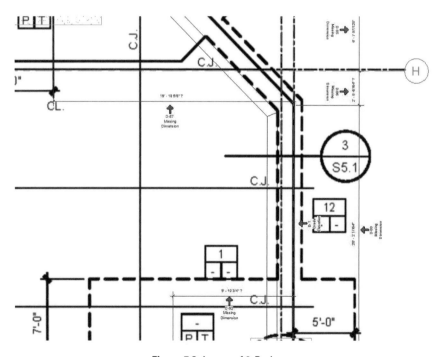

Figure 5.3 Image of 2-D plans.

To-Be Condition

Firms need to have a very clear idea of where they want to be when the implementation is complete. If this general contractor wants to have its own BIM department, then it needs to decide what exactly that BIM department will do. The answers to questions like these are critical in determining if the general contractor will build its own department or if it will outsource this work. If the general contractor chooses to build its own BIM department, then it will have to decide what software will be used. If the organization decides to outsource, then it will be faced with other questions about quality assurance/quality control (QA/QC) and about how many people on the staff will be trained on BIM to deal with the product delivered from the outsource partner. This is also time for the owners to get more control over their projects. They have to determine the who, what, and how of BIM.

As mentioned in the general contractor example, the organization will need to decide what software will be used. The major BIM software products on the market today are Autodesk Revit, Bentley BIM, Navisworks, and Solibri. A big concern for firms must be the interoperability of the software that they choose. They need to know if the subcontractors that they are using can open files in the software they choose while, at the same time, keeping all of the intelligence. This has been a sticky issue in the past between Autodesk Revit and Bentley BIM. When models are created in Revit, they lose their intelligence when they are converted to Bentley BIM. When we talk about "intelligence," we are referring to all of the object-specific data that is in the model. The U.S. Army Corps of Engineers (USACE) primarily uses Bentley BIM on its projects, and it is because of this loss of intelligence (data) in the conversion from Revit to Bentley that the USACE has begun requiring that all models be native Bentley. To be native Bentley, a file must have been created using Bentley rather than converted or exported into Bentley from Revit or another software package. This has made it much more difficult for firms that do not use Bentley BIM to do work on USACE projects. Interoperability, thus, is very important to firms that are trying to decide which software application to use. This is a capital decision for owners as they set up their BIM requirements. Once the decisions are made in reference to the software to be used, the organization needs to determine what types of computers are needed to handle the speed and memory requirements of the software chosen. They also need to determine the types of servers and networks that are needed to support their software choices, file sizes, and file transfer needs.

Staffing will also be a consideration as part of the to-be condition development. Firms have to determine how many modelers will be needed as well as whether this change will affect the number of estimators on staff. Other issues to be dealt with are whether the current CAD drafters can be retrained in BIM and how many of the project managers will be trained in BIM.

> Humans, by their nature, seek purpose—a cause greater and more enduring than themselves. But traditional businesses have long considered purpose ornamental—a perfectly nice accessory, so long as it didn't get in the way of the important things. But that's changing—thanks in part to the rising tide of baby boomers reckoning with their own mortality. In Motivation 3.0, purpose maximization is taking place alongside profit maximization as an aspiration and a guiding principle. Within organizations, this new "purpose motive" is expressing itself in three ways: in goals that use profit to reach purpose, in words that emphasize more than self-interest, and in policies that allow people to pursue purpose on their own terms. This move to accompany profit maximization with purpose maximization has the potential to rejuvenate our businesses and remake our world.[3]

Gap Analysis

One of the first steps in the gap analysis for the general contractor discussed previously is to assess the current state of its hardware. As Juan and Ou-Yang note in their article "Systematic Approach for the Gap Analysis of Business Processes," "Accurate knowledge of the gaps between a company's processes and best practice processes is essential for carrying out these projects successfully."[4] This is true for software and hardware as well. Organizations need to understand where there are gaps with their software and hardware. Firms need to find out if the desktops, laptops, and servers are currently capable of handling the speed and memory requirements of the chosen BIM software. If not, then the systems may need to be upgraded, if possible. If upgrading is not an option, then completely new equipment needs to be purchased. The cost of this equipment and the software could affect the overall implementation schedule. These costs could also determine how big or small the implementation will be. If the costs are too high, then the general contractor may have to scale back or adjust the implementation schedule. Instead of adding ten BIM workstations this year, the organization may decide to add five workstations this year and then another five workstations next year. The beauty of gap analysis is that, if done correctly, organizations can identify the majority of these issues at the outset and adjust their plans prior to purchasing any equipment. Another consideration will be whether their current Internet connection can support the fast transfer of files to subcontractors, architects, and outsource partners.

After the hardware and software needs are determined, the next item to be considered will be training. The organization needs to determine who will be trained. Determine which CAD drafters will become BIM modelers.

There must also be a review of current staff to determine who will be able to make the transition from 2-D to BIM. There may be some people who will have to be let go because their skill set does not fit the to-be condition. For instance, some CAD drafters are not able to or do not want to make the change from CAD to BIM. The general contractor will most likely have to make some hires to fill critical BIM production slots. They must also be prepared to have some staff leave the company voluntarily as "old-guard" employees will not want to make the

A TALE FROM THE TRENCHES

A general contractor in Texas decided that it wanted to start using BIM on its projects. This general contractor decided that its best option was to train its CAD drafters on BIM and use an outsource provider for the BIM heavy lifting. These drafters did not want to make the switch from CAD to BIM. They went through the BIM training, but when they started working with the BIM outsource partner, they began to sabotage the projects and blame the problems on the outsource partner. These drafters would invent problems with the BIM models so that they could continue to provide CAD files. The management did not realize what was happening until their projects were in trouble. It had not occurred to them that their trusted employees would try to sabotage the system.

switch from 2-D to BIM. These people could be very valuable employees, so the general contractor must be prepared if they decide to leave. If these employees decide to stay with the company, then the organization needs to make certain that these employees do not sabotage the move to BIM. If employees leave the company due to the BIM transition, then the general contractor is faced with filling these positions.

The Playbook

Once the gap analysis is complete, firms will want to focus on developing a "playbook" to get from the "as-is" condition to the "to-be" condition. As part of this process, firms will want to avoid creating large three-ring binders with a great deal of information that no one will ever read. We have seen this happen many times with information technology (IT) and human resources (HR) policies that are issued in large three-ring binders. These policy books can be hundreds of pages long, and no one wants to read them. What typically tends to happen is that some employees will try to figure out a way around the policy, especially when it comes to IT policies. The disconnect between the company and the employees is that employees feel that these policies do not really help them do their job. In some cases, they actually view the policies as a hindrance to getting their job done. When these huge policy books are issued, employees tend to flip through them and then sign the last page. In essence, they sign something that they have not read because the company makes them do so. If they did not sign the document, then they could be reprimanded and in some cases even terminated.

Because of the negative connotations associated with the large, thick process and/or policy manuals, the company I work for has abandoned this format in developing its playbooks. My company has found that, much as in sports, our projects are very fluid and things change. Because of this, we have to be prepared for different situations. This necessitates the creation of different playbooks. This approach has been very successful for many firms. When we look at a playbook, there are three main components:

- Input
- Standard processes
- Output

The *input* deals with the "who, what, and when" of a project. In the case of the general contractor that wants to implement BIM, the "who" would cover several groups. The first would be those who will be leading the effort or project. This would most probably be a member of upper management and a group of project managers representing each working group involved. For these purposes, the second group will be those who are currently doing the work and those who will be doing the work after BIM implementation.

In the case of BIM implementation, the "what" includes current staffing levels, skill sets of the employees, and hardware and software capabilities. As mentioned earlier, the organization will need to consider the skill set of each employee. It will also have to perform an inventory of the hardware and software available. This is also the point where the organization will need to determine how much it is willing to spend on this transition. As part of the "what," the organization will need to look at current processes and determine which ones will survive the transition and which ones will be "deconstructed." This is where firms have to delve into the details of what they do and how they do it, so that new processes can be developed and implemented.

The next area to be dealt with in the playbook will be the "when" of the project. Based on the available funds for the project, the organization can begin to plan when the project will be executed. Again, there are several variables that need to be considered. The first would be the skill sets of the current employees. The organization needs to determine if the employees can be trained in BIM or if they will need to be replaced. In order to maximize the benefits and return on investment (ROI) of BIM, the organization should define the time frame for these resources to be retrained or replaced. Again, the question of who will do the work while resources are being trained becomes an issue. How training is accomplished will have a major impact on the "when" of the project. The issue of infrastructure is also critical, as none of the changes can be instituted without the hardware in place to move forward.

As discussed, all current processes must be evaluated and either discarded or retooled for use with BIM. Firms must also realize that it is imperative to develop new *standard processes* for all projects. Organizations should develop standard processes that contain standard definitions. A BIM implementation should be considered for each project and should be subject to the same standard processes that have been developed for other projects.

The *output* of the playbook also concerns the "who, what, and when." In particular, the output addresses

- Project process variability
- Change management
- Building a "vocabulary"
- Training plan
- Business development
- Project executives
- Preconstruction
- Project management/engineering and field staff

Regarding project process variability, firms do not want to develop a playbook that is so specific that no one else can use it. If they do this, then the playbook becomes too constricting and does not help people to do their job. When building a playbook, an organization's knowledge really matters. The organization definitely does not want to have someone with little or no experience developing its playbook because there is a fine line between too much detail and too little detail.

The next area to deal with is change management. The architecture, engineering, and construction (AEC) industry must contend with many different types of changes—from constantly changing weather to incompetent subcontractors. Firms definitely do not want to get halfway through their project, discover that they need to fire a subcontractor because he or she is doing a bad job, and then find out that the subcontractor cannot be fired. It is very important to address change because we know that it is going to happen because it always happens. The playbook addresses these changes in many ways. It could be as simple as "if this doesn't happen, go get a vice president, director, or partner in the organization to get it resolved." The solutions can be that simple. The key is that firms must always have contingency plans for when things go wrong. (See Figure 5.4.)

The next step is building a vocabulary. This is the most important item in the playbook. When dealing with a paradigm shift, it is found that people tend to create new terms. A good example would

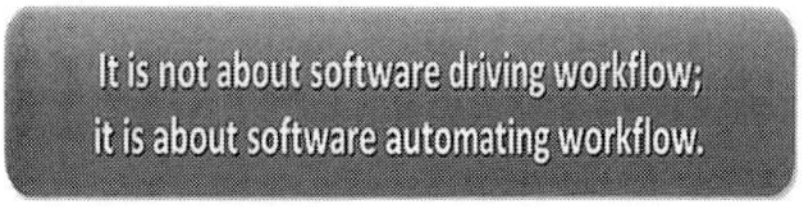

It is not about software driving workflow; it is about software automating workflow.

Figure 5.4 Workflow.

be integrated project delivery. Integrated project delivery (IPD) is a project delivery system that seeks to align interests, objectives, and practices (even in a single business) through a team-based approach. Because of a "shared risk, shared reward" system, IPD provides interesting possibilities for the use of (and discussions about) BIM. In IPD, everyone is supposed to work together; it is viewed as a kind of "kumbaya" agreement. Unfortunately, most people do not even understand what IPD means. The high-level concepts are understood, but an industry-wide vocabulary has yet to be developed. As an industry, we have a very established vocabulary. Requests for information (RFIs), design development (DD), construction documents (CDs), and so on are commonly used terms in the current vocabulary, but we have yet to add to this established vocabulary. Simply ask ten people for their definition of BIM to experience the lack of an established vocabulary. A good example would be a general contractor I talked with recently who was working on an IPD project. He did not really understand what he was supposed to do as a member of an IPD team. Once I explained how IPD works, he asked, "So does this mean I can't beat up on the architect anymore?" It is very important to develop a vocabulary and a glossary of terms for projects so that people understand what things mean. Projects will run much more smoothly if everyone knows and understands the meaning of the content. At the company where I work, we develop a project glossary that includes names, terms, phone numbers, and so forth. Once firms have developed a vocabulary, they have to train their people on it. Having a vocabulary that no one knows or understands is a recipe for disaster, which makes training critical.

Developing a training plan is a key component of the playbook. Everyone needs to understand how to use the playbook. A good example of the need to provide training is the corporate expense report. Most people have had some experience with their accounting department making a change to the corporate expense report. How do they usually make this change? They send out an e-mail and possibly post a message on the corporate intranet with a copy of the new expense report and a message that says this new form must be used starting on a specific date. There is no training on what has changed. Sometimes the form is completely different from before, and yet no guidance is provided on how to fill it out. Invariably, when we turn in our first expense report using the new form, the accounting department will contact us and be upset that we prepared our expense report incorrectly. Could this have been avoided? Absolutely. Would it have helped the accounting department to have a playbook? Absolutely. This applies to projects as well. If we are going to drive standard processes, it is very important that people be trained on them. When an organization talks about training and playbooks, this needs to apply to everyone. For example, the business development team needs to understand what other people in the organization are doing and how this affects the team. We have seen instances where the business development team has not been trained on changes in the organization.

Another very good client uses BIM as part of its sales process. It shows new prospective customers how BIM was used on previous projects and how they can use it on their projects. This organization does not use a PowerPoint presentation or case studies. It walks prospective customers through a model of its last project and shows them where the challenges were on that project and how it dealt with them. This offers a completely new buying experience for clients.

Although the business development team is a hard group to train, by far the most difficult group to train is upper management. As Irving Buchen notes in his article "Paradigm Shift Leadership," "The collaboration of middle managers must be focused on defining the difference of innovation and the need for it to be ongoing." "CEOs must build into their succession plan a retraining effort from which they are not exempt."[5] I have worked for great leaders in my career. Many of them expected more of their employees than the employees expected of themselves. These men were very smart, highly intelligent,

A TALE FROM THE TRENCHES

A good example of this is the head of business development at a huge general contractor who claimed that his organization was doing BIM on every project and that they could do 3-D, 4-D, and 5-D. I asked him how this was possible when he only has a BIM department of five people. His response was that he has a huge BIM department that can take on any job. I then proceeded to tell him that we just finished working on a project with his organization and that there are really only five people in the BIM department. His response was typical: "Well, that's what I was told." This shows that all departments, especially the business development department, need to understand how BIM is actually being used and purposed. Credibility is critical during a technology change.

and very successful. Unfortunately, as the industry changed around them, they communicated change but did not lead by example. The term "eat your own dog food" comes to mind. So when we talk about change, we have different views. In trying to get upper management up to speed on what we were doing with technology and why it mattered, I would also show them what the business would look like in five years and even what it would look like in ten years. This involved some training for my bosses (i.e., the upper management). The problem was that they did not even have the vocabulary yet. This made discussing strategic planning with them very difficult, even though they were very open minded. Their openness to change made it easier for me, but this may not be the case with other companies. This makes BIM implementation that much more difficult, because if the CEO does not care about BIM, then there will not be buy-in from the top. "In order to make this transition work, firms must be able to balance vision and mission. They must have executives and managers aligned in a distributed leadership relationship."[6] Middle managers and project managers need to be able to depend on the CEO and other executives for help; otherwise, the whole BIM implementation is doomed to fail. The transition to BIM is an immense undertaking, and upper management needs to understand how it affects the company in order for the BIM plan to work. BIM buy-in from the top should be implemented no differently from any other strategic initiative. I have heard many CEOs in AEC firms talk about the strategic importance of BIM only to champion the initiative by hiring a college intern to serve as their in-house BIM "expert."

Another very important group is the field staff. We have worked on several IPD projects, and on one in particular, we were brought in as the BIM "mediator." In this case, the general contractor and the architect were having what we consider a "BIM-off" because each thought that its BIM department and BIM model were better than the other's. This was causing serious delays on the project. To end the stalemate, the owner brought us in to manage the BIM process. With our help, the project got back on track. When we got to the field implementation part of the project, we met with the superintendent and started going through Navis and doing training. As part of this process, we referred to IPD, and the superintendent stopped me to ask, "What is this IPD thing you keep talking about?" I explained that it stood for integrated project delivery and that it was the contracting method being used on this job. He asked me to explain what IPD meant. I told him that this was really outside of my scope on the project but if he would buy me a steak and a beer, I would explain IPD to him. He agreed and we went out to dinner and I explained how IPD works. After going through the IPD process, he asked, "So under IPD I am required to be nice to the architect?" This is very similar to the general contractor mentioned earlier who was concerned that he couldn't "beat up" on the architect on his job. The issue here is that no one told this superintendent how IPD works. He did not even understand how he was supposed to issue RFIs in the IPD process. He was very concerned because his organization had standard forms for things but those forms wouldn't work in the IPD process and there had been no training to prepare him. He was also concerned about project meetings. "Who do I invite to the project meetings? Do I invite everyone?" He had no concept of how to execute on IPD. Unfortunately, this isn't that uncommon. The most disconcerting issue is the fact that the project superintendent did not even know that the project was IPD. This was a major failure on the part of his organization. BIM may be the vision of one, but it is tactically the job of many.

Owner demand for BIM has increased 50 percent per year over the last few years and is currently being mandated by several federal agencies (e.g., the General Services Administration [GSA], the USACE, the Naval Facilities Engineering Command [NAVFAC], and the Department of Defense [DOD]).[7] Using the power of BIM will greatly improve the traditional construction process—saving a tremendous amount of time and money while mitigating risk for the project stakeholders involved.

However, it is important to point out that any specific BIM procedures carried out depend greatly on meeting clear, pinpointed BIM objectives determined at the owner level. A BIM model can be used throughout the project life cycle, but the BIM process involved between phases (e.g., design, construction, closeout) depends on the specific BIM goals to be met. An excellent method for the owner to address this is to issue a BIM implementation guidebook, which outlines the owner's BIM objectives, required processes, and accepted methodologies for the project.

Following is a list of several possible ways in which BIM can be used on a project (note that these should be addressed and standardized in a typical BIM implementation guidebook):

1. Use of BIM for more accurate creation of design documents and evaluation of existing systems

2. BIM model and level of detail of existing conditions in architectural, structural, mechanical, electrical, plumbing, fire protection, civil, and other building systems

3. BIM model and level of detail for new construction for all disciplines

4. Constructability reviews, utilizing discrepancy reports, to identify errors and omissions for correction of construction documents prior to construction

5. Utilizing BIM for trade coordination, preparing clash reports (see Figure 5.5), and conducting meetings to present the results

6. Incorporation of shop/fabrication drawings into the model

7. Use of on-site and virtual meetings for driving changes back to the design documents

8. Incorporation of custom Revit files, including new technologies, into the model

9. Spatial validation per Building Owners and Managers Association International (BOMA) standards

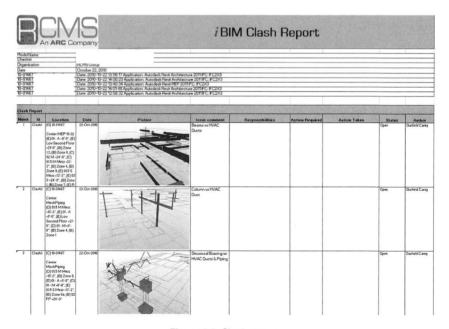

Figure 5.5 Clash report.

10. Circulation validation

11. Energy and related sustainability analysis, including energy estimates and light and acoustic studies

12. 4-D/5-D phasing modeling (i.e., construction sequencing for improved materials staging, scheduling, etc.)

13. Live as-built model updates (via drawings or active, on-site modeling using Vela Systems)

14. Quantity take-offs for improved cost estimating

15. Walk-throughs and animations for trade coordination

16. Facility management (FM) models (using ARCHIBUS, FM:Systems, etc.)

17. Archived BIM model in a specific software format for educational purposes

It will be important to pinpoint the specific BIM objectives that are most important to the owner and to highlight the success of a specific project. Upon award, the owner should determine its most crucial BIM goals and the critical success factors (CSFs) that must be met.

Owners typically spend $100,000 or more for a BIM consultant in order to outline their BIM requirements in a guidebook. As BIM technologies and processes continue to improve, the guidebook must be updated and appropriately "timed" with project delivery in order to match current and future software compatibility needs as well as the skill level of the user base.

Guidebooks can range in complexity and thoroughness, depending on the owner's BIM capability. Some owners may simply issue a one-page "BIM requirement," with bullet points signaling that BIM is required for design, trade coordination, and as-built documentation. While this approach will allow more firms to compete, failure to further specify according to relevant objectives will promote a wide interpretation of these BIM requirements and may actually contribute to poor BIM execution on project.

For example, the following excerpt from a request for proposal (RFP) outlines a very broad, ambiguous BIM requirement:

> Building Information Management Systems: Owner desires to develop a BIM library of existing buildings and projects. The Architect is expected to provide advice and guidance with

respect to provision of construction drawings and as-built information on BIM modeling, utilizing the most current version of REVIT software. All drawings using BIM will be developed using modeling standards, as approved by Owner.

In the case of this RFP, the above excerpt was the only paragraph that stipulated that BIM was to be used on the project. The owner has provided very little information in terms of how the architect, engineers, contractors, and other project stakeholders are to be compliant. The only requirement for BIM submittal seems to be that the architect use Revit to develop its drawings and that it provide "advice" with respect to how to use BIM. This leaves the interpretation of this requirement very open-ended, as there are myriad questions that need to be answered before a submitting firm can be considered compliant with the RFP.

Conversely, several owners have developed BIM guidelines so extensive that while they may limit the resource pool, they will bring forward only the most qualified BIM-enabled firms. For example, the USACE has developed an extensive guidebook that must be adhered to in order for any project member to be considered compliant.

This requirement, known as Attachment F, outlines the USACE BIM requirements and describes the following areas in great detail:

1. Design deliverables
2. Design requirements
   a. Drawings
   b. BIM model and facility data
   c. Industry Foundation Class (IFC) coordination view
   d. Submittal requirements
   e. BIM implementation plan
   f. Model components
   g. Quality control
   h. Design and construction reviews
3. Design state submittal requirements
   a. Submittal requirements
   b. Interim design submittals
   c. BIM and CAD data requirements
   d. Final design submission and design complete submittals
4. Over-the-shoulder progress reviews

5. Final as-builts and CAD data
6. BIM requirements
   a. Architectural/interior design
   b. Furniture/fixtures/equipment (FFE)
   c. Structural
   d. Mechanical
   e. Plumbing
   f. Electrical/telecommunications
   g. Fire protection
   h. Civil
7. Ownership of data
8. Contractor requirements
   a. Construction Operations Building Information Exchange (COBIE) compliance
   b. Electronic exchange
   c. Project scheduling using the model (4-D BIM)
   d. Cost estimating
   e. Submittal requirements
   f. Project completion

Attachment F expands on each item in the preceding list, specifically listing model requirements and submittal procedures. For example, under section 6b, the requirement lists the specific way in which FFE must be presented in the model:

> Furniture/Fixtures/Equipment: 3D representation of FFE elements is preferred. For projects with an extensive systems furniture layout that may impact BIM system performance the Contractor will contact the Government for consideration of 2D representation. The FFE systems Model may vary in level of detail for individual elements, but a minimum must include all features that would be included on a quarter inch (1/4″ = 1′-0″) scaled drawing.

Note the level of detail to which the FFE must be presented in the BIM; otherwise, the BIM will be considered to be noncompliant. Compare this to the first example, which allows the user to interpret what should be included in the BIM.

For an owner, balancing the precision of a requirement with the actual capability of its vendors is an important process. The vendors that can afford to invest in a complex requirement will be few and thus stifle competition.

Educational Leadership

The owner takes on an important role in the new construction ecosystem, as BIM and other emerging technologies continue to improve the building process. Because it is in the owner's best interest to remain engaged with the BIM implementation, the knowledge gained during each project's milestones should continually be applied to future projects in order to continually improve the BIM process.

An owner must take a proactive approach with BIM not only to remain competitive but also to drive competition with bids on future projects. As BIM increasingly becomes an owner requirement, contractors, subcontractors, and other project stakeholders must keep up with the intellectual demand BIM places on an organization in order to remain BIM compliant. A firm's ability to meet BIM requirements will dictate whether or not it can bid on certain projects. If these bidders are eliminated from the pool, costs are driven up due to less competition. Therefore, it also remains in the owners' best interests to continually educate their vendors, which will ultimately further drive quality and efficiency into their projects.

An owner should take the initiative not only to develop internal knowledge about BIM methodologies but also to hire or select key staff members to lead the effort. These personnel, sometimes referred to as "virtual construction directors," play the role of "BIM champions"—continually improving the overall BIM process while proactively contributing to successful project deliveries.

One area in which these BIM champions can help their companies benefit from project to project should include the compilation of a BIM knowledge base. A BIM knowledge base can serve as an internal reference for the owner, including the essential "lessons learned" on each project. More specifically, it should exist as a dynamic set of documents, continually being updated as the owner improves its best practices for hiring BIM personnel, educating the vendor community, and selecting project stakeholders.

The primary component of the knowledge base should consist of case studies, which at a very basic level should include the type of project, the BIM services performed, the ROI analysis, and key take-aways and other lessons learned. An example of a typical case study summary is shown in Figure 5.6.

It should be noted that the case studies can also be used by owners for marketing purposes, showcasing to the public and the AEC community their proactive efforts to use BIM and reduce waste in the construction process.

The case studies should summarize the experience gained using BIM on these projects, and they should be stored electronically for use in future projects. The owner's BIM knowledge then becomes scalable, as new BIM personnel can utilize this reference when executing BIM on a similar project. For instance, the experience in using BIM on a higher-education project (such as that shown in Figure 5.6) can be easily referenced and improved on the next higher-education project.

Educating the stakeholders can be achieved through newsletters, workshops, and even technical training to a specific preselected vendor community (as discussed in the next section).

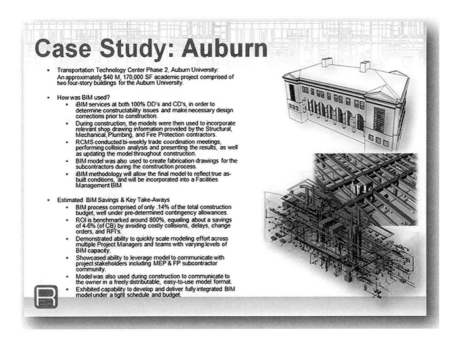

Figure 5.6 Auburn case study.

Preferred Vendor Program

Because project stakeholders can drastically vary in terms of BIM adoption, it is vital for an owner to be thorough in its evaluation of possible vendors. Certain vendors may excel with BIM, while others may overstate their BIM prowess and "scramble" to bring on the necessary staff members, technology, and processes in order to bid on an owner's BIM-required project. Owners are now taking an important step in clean construction by qualifying only BIM-capable firms for their projects.

An owner must not take any contractor or subcontractor's ability to perform BIM at face value. An owner should standardize a method for prequalifying and rating these subs and compile this into a preferred vendor list.

For example, the following outline can be used in a prequalifying document by which vendors can be rated.

List five projects in which BIM was used, including:

- Project name and scope
- Role or involvement with the model
- How BIM was used during each phase of the project
- Estimated savings/loss due to the incorporation of BIM
- Explanation of how BIM will assist in the successful execution of the project
- Résumés/bios of three key personnel responsible for the management and delivery of the BIM model
- Availability for on-site meetings and trade coordination involvement
- Proof of bonding capacity and statement of errors and omissions (E&O) insurance
- Methodology for finding potential RFIs and change orders, including examples of deliverables and an explanation of how these will be used throughout the project to mitigate risk
- Standard for delivering quantity information for use in cost estimating
- Explanation of software/hardware/training requirements in order to utilize and collaborate with the model
- On-site presentation of your RFP response or proposed BIM solution

- Anticipated ROI on the project through the utilization of BIM
- "Value-added" items that can facilitate a quality deliverable and increased communication with the owner

The owner can also standardize this into a preferred vendor database, with a rating system based on BIM compliance and other factors. There can be many other factors that can be considered, with importance shifted toward project objectives more relevant to the specific project or project type (see section i).

BIM Content and Specification Library

As a solid strategy for improving a building's delivery process, an owner can leverage each project for future use by collecting data while standardizing the vendor community BIM methodologies. These models can be leveraged for the owner's "kit of parts"—or content—to be used on future projects. By issuing a specific BIM requirement under the guidebook, the content included with a model submittal can have a specific piece of data attributed to each piece of content that is important to the owner. As more and more projects are submitted, this content library can then be used to standardize— or "prototype"—certain building types, increasing both the bidding and the design cycle for future projects.

As a recent example, I worked with an owner that routinely built high schools. For XYZ High School, the owner specified in the requirements almost all the components that make up a high school, such as light bulbs, standard rooms, electrical panels, and exit doors. For each component, the standard set of data that would need to be included for each "part" was specified in the BIM requirements. Upon completion of the project, the owner required a final model submittal and owned the modeling content library for the high school. This submittal is the first step in standardizing the content library, which will grow and improve upon each completed project.

When the next high school is ready to move forward, the content library can be issued as modeling content with the bid package. Since designers and engineers will have the standard kit, BIM-enabled projects can develop a more accurate cost estimate, bid, or design package. Essentially, the project team will be issued not only a standard BIM process to follow but also the "kit of parts" in which to follow it with. Since each prototype will contain known quantities with pre-determined specific information to be included, it will help to drive down costs and promote competitiveness among vendors.

In this example, the content library (see Figure 5.7) can be considered part of this owner's high school prototype. Specifying the high school prototype on future high school projects will allow for a much more efficient design and construction process, as well as speed up occupancy of the high school. See Figures 5.8 through 5.10 for a BIM of a school.

Figure 5.7 BIM object.

Figure 5.8 A school.

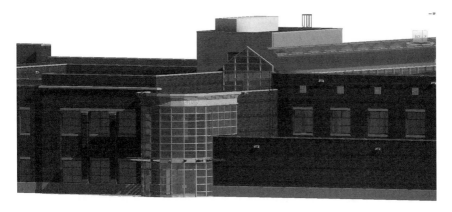

Figure 5.9 BIM showing the outside of a school.

Figure 5.10 BIM showing the inside of a classroom.

BIM Owner's Representative

Many owners recognize the need for BIM but also understand that their vendor community has limited capability. Owners are hiring consultants to represent their interests through the design and construction process. The BIM owner's rep parallels the typical function of an owner's rep but is focused on the end deliverable. The owner's rep ensures that the building meets the owner's requirements while the BIM owner's rep ensures that the virtual building meets the owner's requirements.

CHAPTER SUMMARY KEY POINTS

- Firms must take their overall plan and map it out step by step.
- The first thing an owner must do is determine the as-is condition.
- If a general contractor wants to have its own BIM department, then it needs to decide what exactly that BIM department will do.
- The beauty of gap analysis is that, if done correctly, an organization can identify the majority of the issues at the outset and adjust its plan prior to purchasing any equipment.
- After the gap analysis is complete, firms will need to develop a playbook to get from the as-is condition to the to-be condition.
- The playbook addresses project process variability.
- Case studies should summarize the experience gained utilizing BIM on past projects and should be stored electronically for use on future projects.
- Owners are now taking an important step in clean construction by qualifying only BIM-capable firms for their projects.
- An owner must not take any contractors sub's ability to perform BIM at face value.
- Owners should standardize a method for prequalifying and rating these subs and compile this into a preferred vendor list.
- The to-be condition process is a good time for owners to gain more control over their projects.
- Architects and general contractors are now using BIM because owners are requiring it for their projects.
- General contractors are using BIM for constructability purposes.

chapter

6

Execution

Execution will help you, as a business leader, to choose a more robust strategy. In fact, you can't craft a worthwhile strategy if you don't at the same time make sure your organization has or can get what's required to execute it, including the right resources and the right people. Leaders in an execution culture design strategies that are more road maps than rigid paths enshrined in fat planning books. That way they can respond quickly when the unexpected happens. Their strategies are designed to be executed.[1]

The correlation between time and effort spent in strategy and planning is about a tenth of the effort required for execution. This should be taken into consideration when prioritizing execution. Unfortunately, many organizations exist with a project portfolio of half-baked cakes. Prioritization of execution not only provides bias toward success but also creates an internal view of a pragmatic approach that is easily bought into.

With BIM, there are two different approaches that create a narrow focus with measurable results. These are the enterprise approach and the point solution approach. The enterprise approach requires specific functional leadership and improvement of key performance indicators (KPIs) within a functional unit. The point solution approach is much more focused on solving a specific ongoing challenge. The third approach is the compliance approach, which is not driven by any valued metrics, other than contractual compliance.

Execution can be a resource challenge for many organizations, and it is common to employ consultants with specific experience in executing these strategies.

"Boiling the Ocean" Approach

We will refer to the first approach as "boiling the ocean." In this approach, an organization attempts to do everything at one time. A good example of this would be an organization that wants to start using BIM on all projects at one time. To do this, the organization would have to do several things:

1. Buy the necessary software licenses.
2. Buy or upgrade all of the existing computers to handle BIM software requirements, spreading thin the organization's financial resources.
3. Upgrade the server network to handle the increased storage needs and speed requirements.
4. Train all production resources in BIM. This would also put a strain on the organization's financial resources.
5. Develop processes and procedures for implementing BIM on new projects. This would include quality assurance/quality control (QA/QC) and all other processes and also involve a complete review of all existing processes—a very large endeavor.
6. Train all resources on the new processes and procedures.
7. Retrain the entire sales staff on BIM so that they can successfully secure BIM projects for the organization.
8. Revamp the organization's marketing efforts to focus on BIM. This will involve some training of the marketing group so that they understand what they are marketing.
9. Continue to successfully deliver on current projects while completing steps 1–8.

Obviously, this approach would not be successful. Not only would the organization's financial resources be spread too thin but project management and upper management resources would also be severely strained. The "boiling the ocean" approach would end in ruin, because as the organization would expend great amounts of time and money while simultaneously not delivering on its current projects. Ultimately, the organization would fail because clients would leave when their projects were not completed on time and within budget. The "boiling the ocean" approach is usually used by firms when there has been a lack of planning and strategy.

Enterprise Approach

In an enterprise approach, an organization selects a functional aspect of its business that it thinks BIM will be helpful to and then uses it every time. We have worked with some architecture firms that are using BIM for conceptual and schematic modeling, and they use it for this on every project. They do not get to select projects or use BIM on one or two projects—they use it on every project. Another example would be general contractors that use BIM for trade coordination. They, too, use BIM on every project for trade coordination. By doing this, they can set up standards, processes, and workflow. They can do this because BIM is used the same way on every project. From project to project, they modify the playbook and make updates to the playbook. Because of this repetition, or "muscle memory," they get better at using BIM. By focusing on one area and doing the necessary training and planning, they can get the process right. They do not waste resources trying to do everything at once. They realized that they couldn't get everyone in their organization up to speed on BIM at the same time, so they chose to be more focused in their approach. These firms realized that trying to "boil the ocean," while remaining a money-making and well-respected organization, was impossible.

Point Solution Approach

The point solution approach is best used when trying to solve a recurring or ongoing problem. An organization must first identify the problem and then focus on how to solve that problem using BIM.

Consider a general contractor that typically has a challenge with coordination of heating, ventilating, and air conditioning (HVAC) systems on its hospital projects. This is an ongoing problem and challenge. The key is to focus on solving that problem using BIM. In that process, the general contractor is going to capture, document, and organize its playbook, information, and standards. The organization will use this problem to plan a system. As a result of this focused approach, the general contractor will develop a wealth of great material, information, and processes and can pull the information off the shelf when the next job comes in. By using a point solution approach, an organization can also calculate the return on investment (ROI) more easily because it has a system in place that will help it measure the ROI. Firms need to also understand that they do not have to do everything alone. They can use outsourcing partners for:

- Consulting
- Consulting and co-managing
- Building information modeling
- BIM gatekeeping
- Turnkey operations

Compliance Approach

The previous discussion of the point solution and enterprise approaches has focused on solving problems. These approaches also drive the downstream benefit of knowledge and learning to the organization. Unfortunately, some owners have skipped the learning process and moved swiftly to taking a compliance approach. Compliance is an important aspect of design and construction; however, it may be rash for many owners to take a compliance approach early in the adoption cycle. When an owner pushes compliance on the architecture, engineering, and construction (AEC) community, it requires its vendors to first determine whether they are competent to comply, and, as a result, many vendors may not respond to the opportunity. If the AEC community does not clearly understand and have experience with compliance, they will either invest to comply or simply try to figure it out later after they are awarded the project. Additionally, when owners have not had sufficient experience with BIM, they do not have systems and processes in place to enforce compliance. What many owners do not realize is that their lack of ability to enforce compliance is not a big secret to the AEC community.

In my experience, this has become the norm rather than the exception. In the future, the adoption of BIM will move to a phase in which compliance will be an important aspect. The tools and knowledge will be engrained in the owners' organizations so that they can both require and achieve compliance while meeting the intent of the requirements.

A TALE FROM THE TRENCHES

For example, about a year ago, we received a request from a large general contractor to partner with them to win a government project. We prepared our scope and fee to meet not just the compliance but also the intent of the BIM requirements. The BIM requirements were very detailed, yet conflicted and voluminous. The comprehensive nature of the requirements necessitated a detailed scope and a larger than usual (for a private project) fee structure. The general contractor was awarded the project, and when we followed up with the general contractor, we were informed that they had decided to execute BIM in-house. Besides the disappointment of not being awarded our contract, we were confused by the decision. This general contractor had little experience with BIM and no experience with the specific software that was required by the owner. They expressed their concern over our fee and that, in effect, they had to low-bid the project. The general contractor's plan was to buy the software and "figure it out" on the job with a college intern they had hired. This created even more concern about the project. We then asked the general contractor if they actually thought they could meet the BIM requirements given their lack of experience. They had heard through the grapevine that this owner had no idea how to enforce BIM and that as long as they created a 3-D model that resembled the building, it would pass. The general contractor said that they would take the risk of having to hire us after the fact to meet compliance. We followed up several months later to be greeted by an "I told you so." This was not the last time that we experienced this exact situation. In fact, our sales team will now ask clients if they are seeking to comply with the specifications only or the intent as well. We typically pass on the clients that seek only to comply with the specifications.

CHAPTER SUMMARY KEY POINTS

- The "boiling the ocean" approach could cause a firm's financial resources to be spread too thin. In addition, project management and upper management resources could also be severely strained.

- When using the "boiling the ocean" approach, an organization could fail because clients would leave when their projects were not completed on time and within budget.

- In an enterprise approach, organizations select a functional aspect of their business that they think BIM will be helpful to, and they use it every time.

- With an enterprise approach, organizations do not get to pick and choose projects on which to use BIM; they use BIM on every project.

- The point solution approach is best used when trying to solve a recurring or ongoing problem.

- When using a point solution approach, an organization must identify the problem and then focus on how to solve that problem using BIM.

- As a result of using the point solution approach, firms will build a wealth of great material, information, and processes that they can pull off the shelf for the next job.

- When organizations use the point solution approach, they can calculate the ROI more easily because they have a system in place that will help them measure the return on investment.

- Compliance is an important aspect of design and construction.

- In the future, the adoption of BIM will move to a phase in which compliance will be an important aspect.

chapter

7

BIM Analytics for the Enterprise

As discussed in Chapter 1, the owner plays a vital role in the BIM process on any project. More important, no involvement in a BIM process—or not utilizing BIM at all—can be detrimental to a project from both a time and cost perspective. BIM levels the playing field for the owner, if the owner is not only involved but provides leadership to the process.

Prior to construction, an owner may allocate additional funds to the total construction budget in order to account for unknowns that relate to anticipated risk on the project. Often this risk is associated with the project type, the owner's confidence in the design and construction teams, and how this corresponds to the potential for the project to run over budget. It is vital for an owner to manage these potential cost overruns up front as a "contingency"—hence, the term "fee set-aside." An owner may typically set aside 3 to 5 percent of the total construction budget toward this contingency fee.

More specifically, this potential risk should be associated with several key areas that typically lead to budget overruns: requests for information (RFIs), change orders, system collisions, and schedule delays. Before we analyze the use of BIM to manage any anticipated

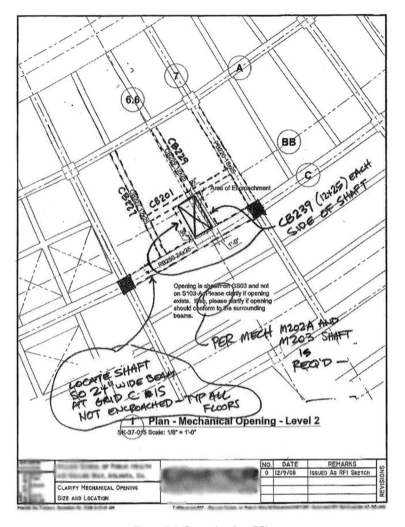

Figure 7.1 Example of an RFI.

risk, it is important to understand these categories and how they relate to a project's budget.

An RFI accounts for the documentation of errors and omissions during the construction of a building. When a contractor can't build or interpret construction drawings correctly, he or she will issue an RFI to the design team. Figure 7.1 shows a typical RFI.

Design teams are familiar with the process of addressing RFIs, but traditionally this process happens at a very inopportune time. Contractors are busy at the construction site when they submit these

RFIs—usually during a process called construction administration (CA). During CA, designers have typically moved on to designing other projects and have exhausted their design budget for the project under construction. Clearing up design issues during CA limits the profitability for the designer and usually isn't given a high priority—causing further delays and costs to the owner.

When using BIM, a virtual construction team will simulate the actual construction process on the computer and compile a list of what it couldn't build virtually. These errors are noted during the BIM process and are then tabulated as a list of discrepancies. This report, called a discrepancy log, is therefore a list of errors and omissions that would have arisen much later in the construction process. By simulating the construction of the building virtually, it can be said that BIM is used to issue an RFI log prior to CA. Generating a discrepancy log puts the RFI process up front, as if the building were built in a "dry run" by a contractor during design. This log is then a by-product of the virtual construction process and represents the analysis of the constructability of contract documents.

Figure 7.2 shows an example of a standard discrepancy log.

A *change order* is work that is added to or deleted from the original scope of work of a contract, which alters the original contract amount or completion date. Change orders are common to most projects and even more so with large projects. After the original scope (or contract) is formed, complete with the total construction budget and the specific scope to be completed, a change order is generated for any work that does not fall within the defined scope.

While some scope modifications are necessary due to owner requests (e.g., major scope changes or additional design features), most change orders are the result of errors and omissions in the contract documents discovered during construction. Using a BIM process on a project will enable the owner and project team to find these potential change orders virtually, prior to issuing costly change orders during construction.

A *system collision*, sometimes referred to as a "clash," describes instances where one system or discipline shown in the contract documents occupies the same physical space as another. For example, it is considered a collision when a mechanical duct is shown as intersecting with a structural beam. If not properly coordinated during design, this will physically occur in the field and result in a costly change order and/or project delay.

Discrepancy Log

Project Name:	Sample Project
Bid Date:	9/11/2009, 11:00 AM
Invitation No:	ASD-CD304
Owner:	Smith LLC
Architect:	Frank Lloyd Left - Architect
RCMS Proj Id:	10-532

Discrepancy Rating (*) Summary

Rating	Count	%
Low	15	47%
Medium	14	44%
High	3	
Total	32	

(*) Discrepancy Rating Legend

Low	Likely to drive RFI with outcomes that require clarifications/confirmation of a condition from A/E. Unlikely to cause field delays.
Medium	Likely to drive RFI with outcomes that require clarifications/confirmation of a condition from A/E. Likely to cause some field delays or drive meetings.
High	Likely to drive RFI with outcomes that could include Design Changes or Field Delays awaiting clarification.

Discipline	No.	Discrepancy	Rating	Sheet#/Section#	Location	TAG #	Modeler
Architectural	1	Entry to Large Toilet Rooms - missing wall opening height, typical	Medium	A-103	Room 325 + 326	Tag 1	CA
Architectural	2	Interior Elevation Tag - drawing coordination error	Low	A-103	Room 336	Tag 2	CA
Architectural	3	Missing Interior Window Tag	Low	A-103	Room 335	Tag 3	CA
Architectural	4	Interior Elevation Tag - drawing coordination error	Low	A-103	Room 342	Tag 4	CA
Architectural	5	Exterior Elevation Tag - drawing coordination error	Low	A-106	North Elevation	Tag 5	CA
Architectural	6	Section Detail Tag - drawing coordination error	Low	A-106	Doorway 609A	Tag 6	CA
Architectural	7	Exterior Elevation Tag - "mirror"	Low	A-107	West Elevation	Tag 7	CA
Architectural	8	Ceiling Height Tag - missing bulkhead information	Medium	A-112	Room 206	Tag 8	CA
Architectural	9	Ceiling Height Tags - more information needed, section callouts needed	Low	A-113	Information Center Ceiling	Tag 9	CA
Architectural	10	Ceiling Heights Tags - contradicting information	Low	A-113	Rooms 337, 338, 339	Tag 10	CA
Architectural	11	Ceiling Height Tags - missing information	Medium	A-115	Corridor 505	Tag 11	CA
Architectural	12	Ceiling Height Tags - contradicting information	Low	A-115	Rooms 509, 521, 522	Tag 12	CA
Architectural	13	Roof Slope Tag - contradicts with sections and elevations	High	A-120	Gymnasium	Tag 13	CA
Architectural	14	Section Tag - incorrect cut directions shown	Low	A-202	2/A-301, 1/A-305 (twice)	Tag 14	CA
Architectural	15	Exterior Elevation - missing parapet height information	Medium	A-204	4/A-204	Tag 15	CA
Architectural	16	Roof Height Information - contradicts slope stated on roof plan	High	A-204	7/A-204	Tag 16	CA

Figure 7.2 Discrepancy log.

Finding collisions is a very basic—but extremely valuable—use of BIM technology. BIM can be used to find hard collisions, which refers to two or more separate systems or disciplines occupying the same space in the building's design. A soft collision refers to a system interfering or clashing within a buffer (or tolerance) set around another system.

A collision can often be cleared up in the field, without a major change order, through some improvisation or immediate correction on the part of the subcontractors. Even when these systems can be rerouted in the field, it still proves costly to the project and adds delays to the construction schedule. A "bird's nest" of systems can create inefficiency in the building's design and add future costs over the building's life cycle.

Figure 7.3 shows a collision as it exists in a virtual space as well as a photograph of the physical correction taken during the building's construction.

For an owner, collision detection and coordination are not part of its responsibility. Generally, an owner should not be part of the process other than quality assurance (QA) oversight. A general contractor can be required to submit a fully coordinated BIM to demonstrate that all coordination has been complete. During the virtual construction process, collisions are noted and tabulated in a collision report, much like the example shown in Figure 7.3.

An obvious detriment to any construction budget is a *delay* due to mismanagement of the project schedule. In fact, failure to manage

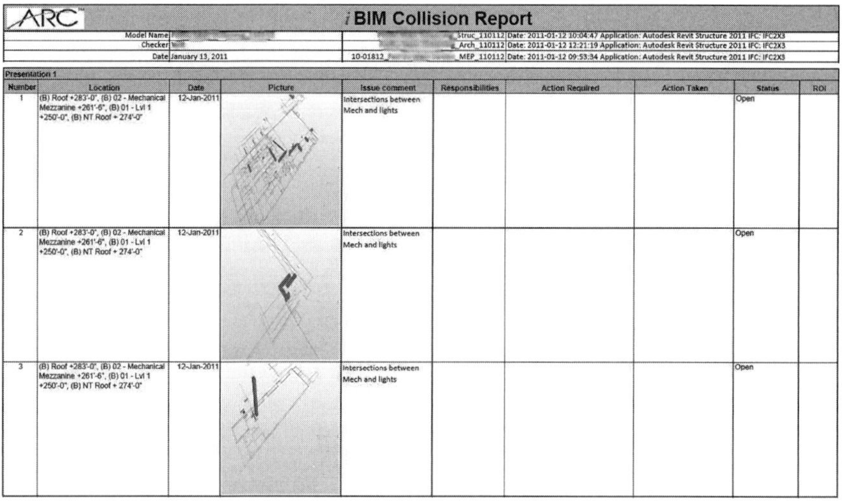

Figure 7.3 iBIM collision report.

the three categories described above often negatively affects this fourth area. Change orders, RFIs, and collisions take time to correct during construction and can produce an "opening-day delay"—an event that may not only reflect pure hard costs but have some intangible detrimental effects as well.

For example, when a high school is delayed during construction and doesn't open on time, there are several hard costs associated with this: lease extensions, taxes, interest on the land, liquidated damages, and perhaps even incremental costs associated with temporary school facilities. However, what may be of more "lost value" could be political. In other words, does it reflect negatively on the school board that the school didn't open on time? Do elected officials suffer when their projects are behind schedule? For other project types—such as hospitals, libraries, and cultural centers (see Figure 7.4)—the lost political capital related to a delay may be even more severe.

In summary, the contingency fee is used to cover anticipated RFIs, change orders, and collisions—all of which result in cost overruns and delays in construction.

Owner ambivalence toward BIM can easily be interpreted as acceptance of spending the contingency fee, which promotes a wasteful and often redundant construction process. Leveraging current BIM methodologies provides the perfect opportunity to simulate the construction process virtually in order to manage this risk ahead of

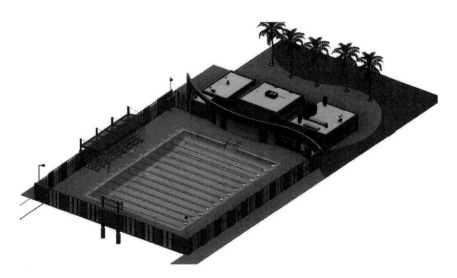

Figure 7.4 Cultural center.

time. In short, if owners choose not to use BIM, they will be "investing" in the process anyway, but with little or no benefit to the project.

One tool that helps owners put their BIM investment into perspective—as it relates to the contingency fee and the construction budget—is a return-on-investment (ROI) analysis.

Measurement: The Return-on-Investment Model

Establishing an ROI calculation prior to embarking on the project is a proven strategy to help align the project stakeholders with the owner's BIM objectives. Because there are many aspects related to construction where BIM can provide value, it is important to select a few key "real world" areas that can be analyzed in relation to cost and time savings. We've found that four of these areas as discussed above—RFIs, change orders, collisions, and delays—provide the most realistic examples that can be benchmarked and calculated during analysis. Ultimately, an ROI model will support an owner's case for implementing BIM and plays a huge role in the ongoing paradigm shift toward virtual construction.

Prior to the project, any ROI analysis is merely hypothetical. In other words, the errors and omissions that we intend to find using BIM have not been found yet. Therefore, the first step toward an ROI analysis is to establish an ROI benchmark.

Benchmarking

Prior to the project, anticipated risk can be quantified in terms of the contingency fee, as described above. In order to best manage this risk up front using BIM, it is important for the owner to determine its expected level of success and to define this as a benchmark so as to be published and reanalyzed upon project completion.

A BIM ROI benchmark can then be defined as the owner's and the project team's expected level of success, measured quantitatively as a goal for each of the four key areas.

In order to demonstrate this ROI process, the following example can be considered a typical K–12 project. We'll use this sample project to establish BIM benchmarks for use in our ROI analysis. The "investment" in this case is utilizing a BIM consultant as a virtual contractor. The purpose of benchmarking is therefore to justify the investment of a BIM process and to quantify the expectation of success.

Example Project: Liberty High School

BASICS

Project Type: Educational, K–12

Construction Budget: $24,000,000 ($300 per square foot)

Square Footage: 80,000

Contingency Fee: $720,000 (3 percent)

BIM Investment (Outsourced): $40,000

Construction Duration: 10 months

The first area we'll analyze as a benchmark is the cost associated with correcting RFIs. In order to determine our benchmarks, it would be useful to look back at similar projects completed traditionally, without the use of BIM.

For instance, on the last high school completed, how many RFIs did the contractor compile during construction administration? Therefore, what does that tell us about this project?

Using our example, we anticipated 400 RFIs would be generated during the CA process.

Second, how many of these RFIs would we hope to manage using BIM? This is the critical benchmark—a factor we can measure later that would indicate success and justify our BIM investment.

In this case, we declared that finding 80 percent of what we would have typically found would be an adequate or realistic definition of success. In other words, if we find 80 percent of our RFIs (320 total) in our BIM process that would have normally been generated during construction, then we would consider our BIM investment appropriate.

Next, let's determine how these RFIs typically affect the project budget. For instance, how much does an RFI really cost the project?

In this case, we determined that each RFI may take an average of five hours to correct using personnel with a typical hourly rate of $80 per hour. Therefore, the RFIs cost us $400 each. This factor will be useful later when compiling our results—measuring our benchmark against the BIM investment.

Figure 7.5 is a sample spreadsheet showing the collection of the RFI benchmark data.

Change Order Costs		
How many change orders do you believe there will be on a project like this?	Anticipated Number	100
What percent of those do you think would be mitigated by using BIM?	% Managed/Mitigated by iBIM	80%
	Number Mitigated Using iBIM	80
What do you think would be the average cost per change order on a project like this?	Avg cost ($) per Change Order	$10,000

Figure 7.5 RFI.

A collision, as defined above, represents systems that were inaccurately laid out in the design, resulting in two or more systems vying to occupy the same physical space. Many times these errors can be corrected in the field but still cause budget overruns and delays. With the help of a BIM consultant, we aim to find these collisions ahead of time, before the subcontractors begin to physically lay out their systems in the field.

For our example, let's anticipate a number for a project of this size, an approximate cost to fix these errors in the field, and an expected level of mitigation.

For Liberty High School, we expect roughly 800 collisions, at a correction cost of approximately $1,000 each. Our goal is to mitigate against 80 percent of these, therefore finding at least 640 collisions prior to erection of these systems.

Figure 7.6 is a sample spreadsheet showing the collection of the collision benchmark data.

Undetected Collision Correction Costs		
How many undetected collisions could there be on a project like this?	Anticipated Number	800
What percent of those collisions do you think would be mitigated by using BIM collision detection?	% Mitigated by iBIM	80%
	Number Using iBIM	640.0
What do you think is the cost to correct an undetected collision?	Avg ($) per Collision	$1,000

Figure 7.6 Collision benchmark data.

Finally, let's analyze delays in the construction schedule attributed to time wasted due to the first three categories.

On a typical high school, a common factor of anticipated "days delayed" is two days per construction month, if built without the use of BIM. This means that for the ten-month construction schedule of our Liberty High School project, we could expect a delay as severe as twenty days. Based on the land, taxes, construction crew size, and so forth, we estimated that each day-long delay on this example could cost the project as much as $20,000.

So, if we consider only the hard costs of delaying the opening of this school, these lost days could prove extremely costly to the project. Again, this calculation does not consider any "revenue model" of the building in question nor does it compute political capital, reputation, or other intangible quantities that could also severely damage the project.

Since we are using BIM on this project, we would like to get back 80 percent of these days lost, or sixteen days.

Figure 7.7 is a sample spreadsheet showing the collection of the "opening days delayed" benchmark data.

Opening Days Delayed by RFI/Change Orders/Collision		
If there is a delay of facility opening, how many days delayed could there be?	Days Delayed	20
If (x)% of the delays were eliminated?	% Managed/Mitigated by iBIM	80%
	Number Using iBIM	16.0
What would the cost be for each day the facility opening is delayed?	Cost per Day Delay	$20,000

Figure 7.7 Benchmark data.

The results of the ROI benchmarks are then calculated for each category. It is useful to compare these benchmarks to the BIM investment as well as a percentage of both the total construction budget and the contingency fee.

For our Liberty High School example, the benchmarking results are tabulated in order to define our anticipated ROI, as summarized in Figure 7.8.

Key Area	Savings	% of Budget	ROI
RFI Process Costs Mitigated by iBIM	$128,000	0.53%	320%
Change Order Costs Mitigated by iBIM	$800,000	3.33%	2,000%
Collision Costs Mitigated by iBIM	$640,000	2.67%	1,600%
Opening Delay Costs Mitigated by iBIM	$320,000	1.33%	800%
Cost Savings Provided by iBIM	**$1,888,000**	**7.87%**	**4,720%**

Figure 7.8 ROI.

Note that from the previously defined "basics" of the school, our BIM investment is roughly $0.50 per square foot, or approximately 0.17 percent of the entire construction budget. This means that the BIM investment makes up less than a quarter of a percent of the entire budget, and significantly less than the 3 percent contingency previously assigned to manage this risk.

Therefore, utilizing BIM on a project with an 80 percent success benchmark, we expect to save

$128,000 on discovered RFIs

$800,000 on mitigated change orders

$640,000 on managed collisions

$320,000 on saved opening days delayed

This means with a $40,000 investment, we expect a roughly 4,700 percent return. More directly, spending 17 percent of the project's budget—at an 80 percent success rate—should yield a return of 7.87 percent ($1.9 million) of the project's budget back into the hands of the owner.

Establishing Key Performance Indicators

Key performance indicators (KPIs) are commonly used by a team to evaluate its success or the success of a particular activity in which it is engaged (see Figure 7.9). Sometimes *success* is defined in terms of making progress toward strategic goals, but often success is simply the repeated achievement of some level of operational goals. Accordingly, choosing the right KPIs for BIM is reliant upon having a good understanding of what is important to the project.

Since KPIs can be used as a way to assess the performance of a project, they are most appropriately defined in a way that is understandable, meaningful, and measurable. In order to be evaluated, KPIs are linked to target values, so that the value of the measure can be assessed as meeting expectations or not.

In order to use KPIs as a tool to evaluate a BIM process, an owner can utilize the benchmark categories as shown during the benchmarking exercise. By measuring the progress of each category, the owner can manage the anticipated risk by comparing the benchmarks with the actual results. Because the process of virtual construction can find numerous issues related to actual construction, it is easy to compare real-world results with previously determined goals. However, because the BIM process discovers construction problems prior to construction, "actual" savings are still considered hypothetical since, theoretically, they have not happened in the field.

KPI Description	Benchmarked Savings	Actual Savings	KPI
Change Order/Collision Costs Mitigated by iBIM	$1,120,000	$1,450,000	129%

Figure 7.9 KPI description.

For Liberty High School, we will establish a KPI for each risk category as a percentage of benchmarked savings versus actual savings. Therefore, meeting a KPI over 100 percent indicates positive performance.

The process of computing the actual costs of RFIs, change orders, collisions, and delays can be highly detailed, but we can apply some "shortcuts" in order to measure our results.

For RFIs, one common way to do this is to review the first discrepancy log issued by the BIM team and assign the estimated hours required to correct each discrepancy. This amount, multiplied by the average hourly rate of the staff, would represent the actual hours required to correct each RFI.

For example, the report (see Figure 7.10) could be annotated by a designer as shown.

Therefore, on the first page of the report alone, there are approximately 80 hours of discrepancy correction. Using the sample designer rate of $80 per hour, this page of discrepancies totals roughly $1,600 worth of correction costs.

For our Liberty High School example, let's assume we found 750 discrepancies, requiring approximately 1,700 hours to correct. At $80 per hour, the computed "actual" result to correct these RFIs is $132,000. Our KPI would then yield a positive result, as shown in Figure 7.11.

Change Orders/Collisions

Depending on the severity of the discrepancies, some may hypothetically result in change orders rather than merely RFIs. Additionally, the collision report will summarize not only potential collisions but major change orders as well.

KPI Description	Benchmarked Savings	Actual Savings	KPI
RFI Process Costs Mitigated by iBIM	$128,000	$136,000	106%

Figure 7.10 KPI chart.

KPI Description	Benchmarked Savings	Actual Savings	KPI
Opening Delay Costs Mitigated by iBIM	$160,000	$120,000	75%

Figure 7.11 KPI 2.

Following the same process, a project team can leverage the collision report to determine the estimated dollar value of construction issues that would have been discovered in the field.

For Liberty High School, let's use our expertise in construction to annotate the collision report with the potential amount each issue would have cost the project.

On the first page of the collision report, we calculated approximately $172,000 in change order and collision savings. Let's assume we follow this process for the remainder of the report, totaling $1.45 million in collisions and potential change orders. Again, this would result in a positive KPI, as shown in Figure 7.9.

(Note that the change orders and collision risk categories were combined for the purposes of this KPI.)

Delays

The "opening days delayed" KPI can be computed with actual results following the completion of the project or by computing saved days at certain milestones. For example, we can establish a KPI to be measured at the five-month point of construction.

For Liberty High School, we would calculate from the project schedule the quantity of days saved at the five-month point. In this case, let's assume we are six days ahead of schedule. According to our benchmark, we anticipated saving eight days by this milestone. (Regardless, if we compute this using our $20,000 per day loss, the ratio will be the same.) Therefore, we can see we are not meeting our KPI, as indicated in Figure 7.11.

There may be other factors contributing to missing this KPI, but this discovery will allow the project team to identify that meeting our schedule savings goal is now critical. The project team members can now identify methods to improve as it relates to this KPI.

Knowledge Base

Once an owner has completed the benchmarking and ROI analysis following a project, this information can be leveraged later during the planning and bidding process for similar projects. It is very useful to tabulate and compile this data into a knowledge base, which will allow the owner and project teams to understand the anticipated risk and expected savings.

By referencing a knowledge base—and, more specifically, a compiled list of ROIs by project type—an owner can drive competitiveness among bidders. Using our earlier example, when another high school project comes along, the owner will be armed with information that will allow it to understand the inherent risks, lower the contingency fee, and reduce the building cost by listing BIM as a requirement. This process is under way with owners at a roughly 50 percent adoption rate.[1]

Following is an example of a knowledge base entry, composed of a tabulated list of the ROIs of sixteen projects, based on project type.

By benchmarking and distributing the ROI analysis for a project, all other project stakeholders can be better aligned with the owner's BIM objectives. During construction, these benchmarks should be used in KPIs in order to measure the team's performance compared to the expectation. Upon completion of construction, the reports derived from the BIM process can be used to quantify the potential costs related to each collision, RFI, and so forth. The preconstruction RFI benchmark should be compared to these quantified reports in order to calculate a true, "hard-cost" ROI.

In summary, the healthy owner will view its investment in BIM as simply reprioritizing funds that were formerly set aside to cover a project's acceptable level of risk: the contingency fee. Not only are there obvious benefits associated with managing this risk up front, but exponential value can then be derived from the by-products of a BIM process. For example, a constructability review model that was used for generating a discrepancy log can later be updated with shop drawings for use as a trade coordination model (see Figure 7.12). This can then be updated at the end of construction and delivered to the owner as an as-built model, which can later be used as a closeout tool and ultimately for facility management.

BIM Owner Research

Whether an owner has already implemented BIM or is in the early stages of adoption, new applications, tools, and methods are always being developed. Creating a structured method of researching, summarizing, and publishing information for stakeholders is an ongoing process. Additionally, researching within an owner organization for process improvement ideas is beneficial. Many of the stakeholders

Figure 7.12 Shop drawings for use as a trade coordination model.

197

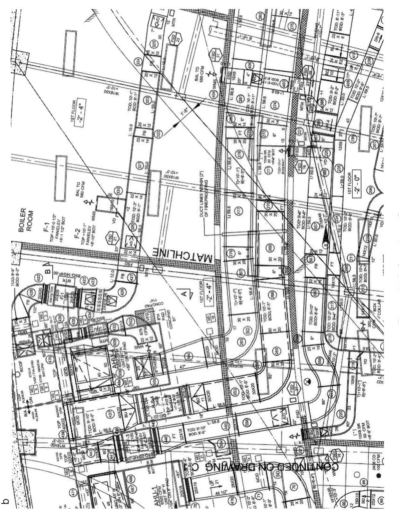

Figure 7.12 (continued).

within an owner organization have significant institutional knowledge but may lack knowledge of BIM and other advanced technologies. The process of researching and publishing information engages the community as well as provides a forum for feedback. This process is typically driven by an executive sponsor (or his or her proxy) within the owner's organization.

Successful implementation of BIM requires engagement of stakeholders at all levels. The champion of the BIM initiative should view the stakeholders as his or her customers. BIM is being implemented to improve the efficiency of the stakeholders while benefiting the enterprise and the champion. Having a customer-oriented attitude drives the development of the appropriate requirements as well as the use of BIM. This requires finding the "voice" of the customer. The voice of the customer becomes the driver to develop a BIM strategy that will be accepted.

While we have referred to stakeholders as a broad base of the user community, it is important to specify user roles. User roles vary by their function and/or functional role, technical capability, and authority. The functional role of a user should be easily developed. This would be maintenance, finance, construction, and so on. Most mature owner organizations have these functional roles defined and published in job descriptions, organization charts, and job titles. If these do not exist, it is important to develop the functional roles of the organization. Also, keep in mind that these functional roles should be predicated on their functional role in using BIM and not on their functional role alone.

The technical aspect of the role is based on both computer technology aptitude and domain expertise. The priority should be domain expertise followed by computer technology aptitude. It is difficult to teach an individual experience with mechanical systems. Domain expertise is experienced based and not classroom based. BIM processes, methodologies, and software applications can be taught to a person with domain expertise. One of the major areas of contention with BIM is the difference between a BIM user and a BIM author. The current condition in the market is to believe that everyone should be a BIM author and expert. My view is that BIM is much like spreadsheet software applications. In surveying a room at a recent BIM executive briefing, I asked a group of attendees if they knew Excel. Everyone raised his or her hand. Then I asked who would like to come up to the front and show us how to build a pivot table and connect it to an external Open Database Connectivity (ODBC) source.

Every hand in the room went down, except for one of my colleagues (he just wanted to show off). The point is that not every user of BIM will be a BIM author, nor should they be a BIM expert. It may not be a requirement of their functional role. The other example that is used frequently in working with owners is the idea that because the World Wide Web is used for shopping, it does not mean that every customer needs to know how the e-commerce Web site was built or its database structure. The 3-D visualization aspect of BIM provides an interface for the user, which, if implemented correctly, creates an environment where everyone would use BIM technology no differently than they use a Web browser.

For example, who would you rather have prepare your taxes: a certified public accountant (CPA) who knows the tax code or a person with no experience with the tax code but who knows how to use tax preparation software?

This is happening today when an owner is engaged in the process and is driving the process. Do not be discouraged with the technical elite in the organization. This is also the broken system that exists within the architecture, engineering, and construction (AEC) community. BIM is being driven by staff that does not even know how to design or build a building.

Authority is a critical aspect of user roles. Authority is the permission set to view, edit, and modify information in BIM. This is similar to security permissions but should be developed based on the user's function and capability. The authority of a user should also be backed by an authoritative process. If a user has the ability to add and modify data, a process by which the data change is approved is critical. The lack of authoritative process can be seen on many corporate network drives. The multiple versions of documents that are in progress and the general disarray of most corporate networks are symptomatic of an insufficient authoritative process. Authority is not a democratic process due to corporate policy or compliance initiatives (such as the Sarbanes-Oxley Act). Some users are more important than others and require a higher priority than others.

A role is not a person or people. This is a concept that can be very confusing for some organizations. Roles should be developed independent of organizational charts, job descriptions, and specific individuals. Developing user roles takes time and is equally as important. Developing the user roles early in the process drives the structure by which the voice of the customer is developed. In other words, if the "customer" is not defined at the outset, then developing his or her voice is impossible. The initial draft of roles should be a long list to start. The reason the list will be long is because it will likely be based on the people and not the role. Once the master list is developed, then grouping roles based on commonalities will shorten the list. Once a final draft of user roles has been completed, it is sent to the user community to be socialized for final feedback. Without a clear explanation of the difference between "roles" and "people," this could be a long, drawn-out process, when, for instance, Steve from finance won't rationalize why he has the same user role as Becky in maintenance.

Upon completion of the user roles, each user will require a representative. This representative is typically self-evident in most organizations. Key attributes include an overall understanding of the organizational challenges, intellectual curiosity, and time availability. These user representatives will be incorporated into a committee, team, focus group, and so on, depending on the organization's cultural vocabulary. A user representative should be included from each role.

The BIM Champion

Assignment of a BIM champion can be a challenge. The BIM champion serves as the main interface between the user representatives and the executive sponsor. The responsibility of the BIM champion is to develop an enterprise program that meets the objectives of the executive sponsor and the requirements of the user community. The ideal BIM champion has great clarity in the executive sponsor's vision while having the intensity to be effective in working with the user community to drive enthusiasm. Beyond a great attitude, the BIM champion must have effective communication skills, both in written and verbal form, and attention to detail. Subjectively, the BIM champion must also have an open and responsive demeanor to work well with others. This is the challenge of assigning a BIM champion. Assuming that this person exists in an organization, the likelihood that he or she will be available to support the BIM effort will be challenging. The BIM champion is probably highly effective in his or her current role, and building a case for their assignment to the BIM initiative requires development of a compelling argument. This process involves interaction by the executive sponsor with their peers. In conjunction with the predicted ROI models based on process improvement, the executive sponsor can drive a compelling argument.

202 BIM Analytics for the Enterprise

The single focus of the BIM champion is to develop the voice of the customer. This voice will be incorporated into a market and technical requirements definition analysis, described later in this chapter. Once the BIM champion has been selected, the process of finding the voice of the customer can begin. Gathering these requirements has two distinct benefits. The first is that the BIM champion hears firsthand the users' requirements. Second, it becomes a platform for the user community to learn about BIM and drive excitement. A BIM champion will encounter resistance from the user community at times because they "do not have time" and preparedness becomes a focal point.

Research Methods

The following tactics form the basis for eliciting information and experiences from the user community to develop the voice of the customer.

Surveying the marketplace and developing white papers that communicate what similar owners are doing with BIM as well as tracking industry trends is a good place to start. Much of the information can be found on the Internet, from application providers to industry groups. Although researching the various software applications can be time consuming, it is necessary. While there are definite market leaders, depending on the specific requirements, a more specialized application may be more suitable. Organize this information into a product matrix and develop an advantages/disadvantages matrix. Most software vendors and consulting companies have published white papers, Webinars (Web-based seminars), and frequently asked questions (FAQs) on their Web site. Always keep in mind that these are published by the vendor's marketing department and, as a result, may be biased.

Surveying the user community is beneficial to determine the current interest in BIM, operational challenges, technology exposure, and so forth. Designing a productive survey does take some time, but executing a survey is easy using e-mail and Web-based survey systems. The process of developing the survey will challenge the BIM champion's understanding of the vision. Also, always test the survey out with a colleague prior to distributing it to the user community. Discovering that a question either does not make sense or can be answered ambiguously after having sent out 100 surveys loses credibility with the user community.

Following is an example survey.

Example Survey

A. Is your facility maintenance outsourced or do you perform this function in-house?

B. Please mark the services you perform for your operation and maintenance of equipment:

- ☐ Preventive
- ☐ Predictive/proactive
- ☐ Reactive

C. Planned events:

1. If you want to schedule a maintenance task for damper lubrication:
   a. How do you determine the frequency for adjusting or lubricating dampers: D, W, M, A?
   b. Do you log or maintain the equipment's run-time database for evaluation that could help in better prediction for future maintenance? If your answer is yes, then how do you log this information?

2. How do you track data for preventive maintenance scheduling? Example: Filter changes:
   a. Who creates the work order and tracks the equipment to be scheduled?
   b. Who allocates resources and defines the schedule for changing the filter at set intervals?
   c. How do you know the correct filter is installed? Do you have a manual available for verification?
   d. Does the filter need to be purchased? If so, who approves the purchase order?
   e. Who completes the work?
   f. How do you record this information in your work order history?
   g. What is your next step?

3. How do you manage your space reconfiguration for a new hire?
   a. How do you track and assign FFE (furniture/finishes/equipment) with respect to the hire's hierarchy?
   b. How do you determine what cubicles and rooms are connected to which network? Are the data, power, and voice connections set up in all those cubicles before assigning the new hire?

4. If you are planning a renovation/extension of your office spaces on the second floor:
   a. Do you have all the drawings with the most current updates?

b. How do you determine the location of all mechanical, electrical, and plumbing (MEP) pipes and ducts above the ceiling and below the floor?

c. Do you have all the specifications, warranty information, service contracts, spare parts, purchase date, and expected lifetime data gathered together for emergency management?

5. Do you have a distributive/alternative work arrangement (DWA) available at your workplace?

☐ Yes

☐ No

If you answered yes, then please answer the following questions:

a. Do you provide furniture and other assets to your employees working from distant places?

b. How do you track the assets distributed to your employees? Do you know how many chairs and desks you currently own?

c. How do you schedule your maintenance on those assets, if required?

6. Do you track your energy consumption and perform energy benchmarking?

☐ Yes

☐ No

a. Who plans and budgets the energy consumption bills?

b. Who pays the energy bills each month? How is this information passed along to the facility management team?

c. What steps will you take if you see a progressive increase in your bills? Please mark the steps you are likely to follow:

☐ Perform a benchmarking to find out how high your bills are with respect to others. Do you have all the data required for benchmarking?

☐ Check all types of fixtures being installed and their energy consumption. If so, how?

☐ Perform maintenance on your equipment to check its performance. If so, is this for all equipment?

☐ Check your building insulation.

☐ Minimize the energy consumption by reducing the load.

7. How do you plan your facility budget for operation and management? Please mention people and processes involved for each step:

a. Establish facility goals and objectives.

b. Capture and analyze data.

      c. Analyze and interpret data.

      d. Create and test alternatives.

      e. Develop strategic plan and budget.

D. Unplanned events:

  1. How do you manage your reactive maintenance?

    a. Employees complain the office is too hot or too cold:

      i. How is the work order placed?

      ii. Who receives it?

      iii. Who allocates the resources: time, money, personnel?

      iv. What is the turnaround time?

    b. Light bulb burns out and needs to be replaced in the administrative office:

      i. How is the work order placed?

      ii. Who receives it?

      iii. Who allocates the resources: time, money, personnel?

      iv. Does the room nomenclature match your database: room number, floor?

  2. How do you plan for unplanned occupancy/vacancy?

    a. If DWA is allowed and all the employees working from alternative work-places show up together one day and there are not enough hot-desking spaces assigned, how would you manage and assign the spaces?

  3. How would you manage the unplanned configuration of a room from a regular employee room to a highly secure room:

    a. Track the door hardware type.

    b. Implement new security system—access codes.

  4. Suppose you have a water fountain leak after a long weekend. You come back after your vacation and find water accumulated near the workstations.

    a. How would you handle the following work tasks:

      i. Do you have a plumbing plan with all the information required for repair or replacement?

      ii. Do you have manufacturer and warranty information accessible?

      iii. Is the water fountain still under warranty? If yes, who installed it and on what date was it installed?

      iv. If the warranty has expired, what is the replacement cost? Is the cost budgeted in your annual facility budget?

      b. Ceiling tiles/grid, wall finishes, insulation, and carpet:

         i. What kind of ceiling tile was installed?

        ii. Do you have all the color codes, and manufacturer's information, warranty, and replacement cost?

       iii. You need to replace a rusted ceiling grid due to a leak. Do you have in-house resources to address this issue?

       iv. Do you have the contact information for the contractor who installed it?

      c. How do you plan to move all your personnel in that area and assign them new work spaces while you deal with this situation?

         i. Do you know how many extra chairs you have in storage, if any?

E. What is your biggest facility challenge? Please explain your answer or give examples.

  ☐ Maintaining facility budget

  ☐ Asset maintenance and management

  ☐ Disaster management planning/emergency preparedness

  ☐ Other

Workshops and seminars can be an effective way to gather information from the user community in a structured but time-constrained manner. These meetings can be designed and facilitated by the BIM champion but, in my experience, are most effective when facilitated by a third party. This third party can be a consultant or an internal staff member with facilitation experience who is not engaged in the BIM initiative. The single biggest challenge of running a workshop is balancing a collaborative environment without going off the topic. Developing some basic ground rules is a great start. Some simple rules include staying on agenda, allowing one person to speak at a time, banning phones/computers (unless someone is transcribing), and planning for a number of breaks and returning from breaks on time. A meeting facilitator is a great help in making workshops run smoothly.

Developing a list of the challenges incurred while using the current systems should be considered. The system is a business system and not necessarily a software system and can be developed by reviewing work order logs, RFI reports, maintenance budgets, and so forth.

User interviews are required as well, and they can be challenging. They can be time consuming for both the BIM champion and the user. My experience is that these become low priorities and are subject to constant rescheduling as more urgent issues arise for the user. It is not reasonable to interview every user in most cases, so use one-on-one interviews as a follow-up tool to workshops, seminars, and surveys.

Shadowing users during the day is a great way for the BIM champion to "experience the user's daily reality." Selecting days that allow the BIM champion to glean as much information as possible about the people, processes, and platforms that a user encounters in a day provides insight that cannot be sourced anywhere else. During the workday, be sure to suggest ways in which the user's job could be more effectively performed if he or she had BIM data. This creates context for the user regarding the application of BIM technology to his or her job and demonstrates the benefit that he or she may reap. In my experience, this has been the most enjoyable and productive use of my time. It is common to receive a call a few days later from the user. The user starts to develop his or her own ideas and build a dialogue with the BIM champion.

Summary of Information

The amount of information gathered from the user community will be vast. Developing a summary of the information gathered and organizing it into a digestible format requires a great deal of effort. Once the summary is developed, it should be sent back to the user community for confirmation. The information can be organized in the following format:

- Executive summary
- BIM mission statement
- BIM vision statement
- BIM objectives (high-value targets)
- User role definition
- Users
- Research methods
- Use cases
- Business rules (internal and external)
- Constraints
- Data standards
- Quality definition

The *executive summary* is beneficial to those who may not be in direct contact with the user community. The need to receive information in a nutshell is important within the user community as well, especially for those who did not have time in the first place.

The *BIM mission statement* should be developed based on feedback from the user community and with heavy input from the executive sponsor. It should not be longer than a few sentences. It should also have a balance between being "high level" and true tangibility. Following are a few examples:

"Improve construction schedules by 10 percent by 2012."

"Reduce maintenance expenses by 20 percent by 2013."

"Create flexibility in our workspace to improve our employee productivity in our new facility."

"Provide transparency for our capital projects to our constituents on a monthly basis."

I have had to create more than twenty mission statements in my career, and this has proven to be one of the most difficult processes. It is also not a task that can be scheduled and becomes a bit organic. The mission statement is critical about the current state of the organization and a near-term goal to improve the business.

The *BIM vision statement* is a long-term view of the organization. The time frame associated with the BIM vision statement is three to five years. Some examples might include the following:

"BIM will be the platform by which we manage all of our facilities."

"Everyone in the organization will become BIM enabled."

The vision statement sets the tone for the future of the organization and provides the staff with an outlook of their importance. Like the mission statement, the vision statement will require tremendous input from the executive sponsor.

BIM objectives should consist of three (typically) to five items. These are tangible objectives with near-term goals. I often refer to these as the high-value targets. The BIM objectives will become the proof of concepts (POCs) for the BIM initiative. The BIM objectives are defined, BIM strategy in order to meet those objectives is developed, and an implementation plan is documented. BIM is executed based on the implementation plan, and the results are reviewed against the stated objectives. This POC will give the BIM champion as well as the user community the ability to experience BIM in a hands-on, relevant approach within the context of enterprise projects with which they are familiar. This experience will bring clarity to both the opportunity as well as the limitations of BIM. Applying this knowledge to the enterprise BIM initiative mitigates risk and refines the definition of the user requirements. Following are some examples of well-constructed BIM objectives:

> "Coordinate MEP systems on the City High School project prior to selecting a general contractor."
>
> "Predict the majority change orders prior to bidding on Wally's Grocery Store in Astoria."
>
> "Create a facility management model that the maintenance personnel can use."

User roles should be defined and documented. These are developed from the research process. By providing this to the user community, it assists in providing clarity to roles versus people. Examples include:

- HVAC model author
- HVAC data administrator
- HVAC maintenance manager
- BIM Content manager

Research methods that were utilized in the findings are important so that the user community understands the background by which the conclusions were drawn. This also becomes a platform to recognize the user representatives who contributed to the effort and to create the initial steps of buy-in. The user community begins to become more engaged in the process.

Use cases are documented scenarios by which the user community will use BIM in the enterprise. These are specific operational tasks that a specific user performs. The majority of these are provided either by the user community in workshops or by shadowing. Taking the use case and applying BIM to it as a future state provides the user a specific application of BIM. As an example, let's look at the use case that begins with *I need to replace a light bulb . . . .*

Current Condition

1. Steve receives a request to replace a light bulb via phone from the accounting department.

2. Steve walks across campus to the accounting department.

3. Steve meets with the requestor and asks to be shown which light fixture is in question.

4. Steve realizes that the light fixture is in a position that requires a lift. It also requires floor protection. He is also not sure of the replacement bulb type.

5. Steve goes back to his office to schedule a maintenance worker, a lift, and floor protection.

6. Once scheduled, the maintenance worker radios Steve to let him know that he needs to order a specific bulb.

7. Steve orders the bulb and reschedules the replacement upon receipt.

This is an actual use case that an owner provided to us.

Future Condition

1. Steve receives a request to replace a light bulb via phone from the accounting department. While on the phone, he pulls up the BIM in which the accounting department resides. He asks the caller for a general location and confirms that it is the fixture next to Suzy's cubical.

2. Steve does a quick measurement in the BIM and realizes that he will need a lift. He clicks on the floor and realizes that it will need protection. He then clicks on the fixture and queries the light bulb type. He does not have the light bulb in stock and has to order it.

3. Upon receipt of the bulb, Steve schedules the lift, protection, and maintenance worker to replace the bulb.

These use cases assist the user community in visualizing their current work effort and how it could change for the better. By providing this in document form, the user has the ability to provide feedback and validate the probability of actualizing the future use case. The above example is a simple use case that yields significant chatter: "If it takes this much work to replace a light bulb, and BIM is optimizing simple work, what about major maintenance issues?"

In more complex owner organizations, a use case diagram may need to be created to fully explain visually a complex workflow.

Business rules address the authoritative processes that exist internally and externally to an organization. These are the conditions that will be applied to a process. In most owner organizations, these rules are procurement related or are design change requests, product submittal approvals, and so forth. In some cases, there could be external compliance criteria such as the Sarbanes-Oxley Act. For example, in the case of a design change request, an owner may authorize the request, but the engineer of record must make the change and submit it. The owner does not have the authority to make engineering design changes that require the seal of a professional engineer.

Constraints are a reality of any current or future system. I typically categorize constraints in terms of the three Ps discussed earlier in this book. Considering the technical skills required by the organization's staff could be a constraint. As an example, perhaps our maintenance department does not even know how to use a computer. In terms of process, the ability to change an institutionalized process could be a constraint. As another example, our executives call the maintenance department and ask us to come to their office. They will not change this process. A platform example could be when the system requirements of a desktop computer for using BIM exceed what is currently available; that is, "the maintenance department has a basic computer system that will not support BIM."

Data standards were discussed previously in Chapter 3. Incorporating the data standards in this document provides an opportunity for users to provide insight and to test the validity of the standards that have been developed. In some cases, when the data standards provided by the software application are used out of the box, the user community will quickly provide feedback. For example, the data standard that is utilized out of the box and is derivative of UNIFORMAT (see Figure 7.13). The construction department organizes all of their budget and estimating data in their own version of MasterFormat in their project accounting system. The user representative from the construction department would provide feedback regarding the conflict.

Determining the *quality* of the data should not be a subjective exercise. Documenting the expectations of quality in the BIM process is critical and routinely overlooked. The typical view is "if the BIM looks right, then it is right." Review of the data and data validation

Figure 7.13 Tables of UNIFORMAT.

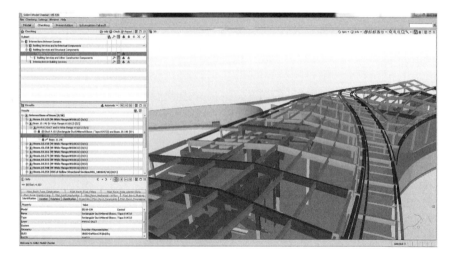

Figure 7.14 Model-checking routine.

is rarely executed. The user community will propose quality attributes that are subjective (easy, simple, reliable) or superlative adjectives (every, all, any). Developing quality goals that can be verified by either human logic or system logic should be defined. For example, the BIM might include an Install Date field for building products that are installed. A model-checking routine would be executed to verify that the Install Date field is not empty (null). Figure 7.14 shows a model-checking routine.

Findings and Conclusions

The development of findings and conclusions requires special attention. The BIM champion must focus on the communication of his or her efforts to all of the stakeholders, including the AEC ecosystem. Change of any kind is a process that challenges many individuals, typically driving a negative outlook. Knowledge and understanding are the foundation of ensuring that change is viewed with a positive outlook. The BIM champion is an agent of change and communication is the most effective tool available. While the BIM champion's work effort to this point has been quite extensive, the development of findings and conclusions in some cases can account for up to 30 percent of the total work effort. The reason for this work effort is due to the fact that individuals learn in many different ways. In order for the knowledge to become engrained in the organization, the findings and conclusions must be communicated by these different methods. Typically speaking, individuals are either visual, textual, or verbal learners. This is further segmented by time availability and attention span. Delivering the findings and conclusions requires keen insight into the types of learners that exist within the stakeholder environments.

The findings should be a clear summary of the research and data derived from the research process. The conclusions should be an interpretation of these findings, described in summary form, along with an explanation of the positive outcomes and the opportunities for improvement.

A TALE FROM THE TRENCHES

My first experience as a management consultant was an internal role in a telecom consulting business. My role was to assess and review potential acquisition candidates, use internal resources to assess viability, and then present my findings to the executive leadership. The executive leadership, in turn, presented the opportunity to the board of directors for approval. This process took place in approximately fifteen days. The key aspect to a potential acquisition (besides the financial metrics) was whether it would be complementary or additive to our current product portfolio. This involved creating a strategic plan and a positioning statement. Because internal resources were used to evaluate these companies, business unit leaders were exposed to these opportunities early in the process. Therefore, every acquisition put these leaders on the defensive and created a negative outlook. Fear that the new company would be purchased and their role would change, that the new company's product was better than their product, that management of the new company was superior, and so on were the first things that they would consider. As we moved closer to the acquisition becoming more probable, I had to communicate the strategy and positioning to many stakeholders. This was my first experience with "different" learners.

- The CFO wanted extensive data and details, typically in spreadsheet format.
- The head of marketing wanted an extensive document in a more textual form (formatting was important).
- The COO wanted the summary in PowerPoint with no more than five slides (his position was that if it could not be communicated with five slides, then there was not enough critical thought applied to the assessment).
- The CEO needed presentations and face-to-face verbal presentations not only to have clarity but also to drive enthusiasm surrounding the opportunity to present to the board of directors.
- The business unit leaders needed several collaborative white board sessions with detailed mapping of the integration and organization structure.

CHAPTER SUMMARY KEY POINTS

- The owner plays a vital role in the BIM process on any project.
- If an owner is not involved in the BIM process, it can be detrimental to a project from a time and cost perspective.
- An RFI accounts for the documentation of errors and omissions during the construction of a building.
- When using BIM, a virtual construction team will simulate the actual construction process on a computer and compile a list of what it could not build virtually.
- A discrepancy log is a list of errors and omissions that would have arisen much later in the construction process.
- A change order is work that is added to or deleted from the original scope of work of a contract, which alters the original contract amount or completion date.
- A system collision describes an instance where one system or discipline shown in the contract documents occupies the same physical space as another.

- Finding these collisions is a very basic but extremely valuable use of BIM technology.

- An obvious detriment to any construction budget is a delay due to mismanagement of the project schedule.

- Prior to the project, anticipated risk can be quantified in terms of the contingency fee.

- KPIs are commonly used by a team to evaluate its success or the success of a particular activity in which it is engaged.

- One common way of computing the actual costs of RFIs is to review the first discrepancy log issued by the BIM team and assign the estimated hours required to correct each discrepancy.

chapter

8

Summary

Building information modeling (bim) is the single most transformative technology for the building industry. All owners easily envision the benefit and opportunities that exist from leveraging BIM. These opportunities are also fraught with challenges and obstacles that the industry has never experienced before. The high degree of failure of BIM implementation demonstrates that applying many of the old principles to BIM has not been successful. The most common old principle is that BIM, like computer-aided design (CAD), is a technology that should be explored and managed by an information technology (IT) department. This drives the highest degree of failures. BIM is a great catalyst for an owner to drive change in its vendor community and in the industry as a whole. Many owners believe that their vendor community of architects, engineers, general contractors, and subcontractors have extensive experience with BIM and are leveraging their expertise. In reality, very few have significant expertise and are learning on the job. More simply put, the "R" in return on investment (ROI) accrues to the organization that makes the "I." BIM is about owners transforming their methods of developing and constructing building projects. While many of the complexities that have been outlined in this book can seem to be overwhelming, it is equally as overwhelming for the vendors that serve the owner.

The difference is that the vendor community does not have much to lose or gain by implementing BIM. The analogy of the travel agency business is the most relevant for an owner. The travel agents had powerful data at their fingertips. They used this data for their benefit, not for the benefit of the consumer. When Internet technologies drove transparency and accessibility of this data to the consumer, the game changed. The power of data and technology allowed consumers to make decisions to their benefit.

The majority of the architecture, engineering, and construction (AEC) community fear the true power of BIM due to self-preservation anxiety. The few that have made the investment in BIM understand that changing their business model is essential. They recognize that the change of their business model can either be voluntary or involuntary. Many architecture firms are struggling with transforming their business and understanding their true value creation. Many firms believe that they are in the business of producing construction documents. Others believe that they are advisors to the owner, but still price their fees based on construction costs. The alignment of risk and reward does not exist. The concept of ROI does not exist. There are two types of professional service businesses. One is essentially contract labor, and the other is value based. Most architecture/engineering firms would put themselves in the value-based category, but their fee structure and business model do not support this. They are still highly focused on billable hours and utilization. The transparency that BIM provides to the owner and the productivity gains in production will drive the revenue from being a contract labor model to being a value-based model. Like many professional service businesses, the leverage in profitability is made by the production staff. The scale in revenue generation is based on staffing leverage. BIM will drive the production time to a tenth of its current state. The leverage of revenue in production staff will be nonexistent. Much like the software industry, a firm that is value based must invest in the development of proprietary technology and processes. The monetization of this value is driven less by the expertise of the individuals in the firm and more by implementation of this expertise into systems. Monetizing a system is based on the value creation to the consumer. The concept of a single client paying for the investment of a system is not realistic. Build it once and deliver many should be the vision. In many firms, the rebuttal is that every project and client are different. A truly experienced professional is able to see the trends of commonality and design in a system. A value-based model provides scalability in revenue and much higher margins. The owner is willing to pay more based on the value the service provides. This shift will require professional service firms to throw out their old business metrics of staff size and utilization. A new vocabulary of revenue, product management, and research and development will be acquired. When a CEO of an architecture firm is asked about the size of the firm, the response is typically X number of people. The metrics of $250,000 of billings per head moves to $1 million per head. Owners want value, not contract labor. The professional service firms should change their model to create value.

The contractor community continues to understand the value drivers of the owner. The transparency of BIM and other advanced technologies is driving the contractor community to much more open pricing models. While labor is a significant contributor to construction costs, the materials cost and waste of materials is much more significant. BIM will continue to drive waste out of the construction system and these savings will eventually be passed on to the owner. Currently, these savings are being captured by the contractors to fund their investments in BIM and other technology. BIM will drive the construction industry from accuracy to precision with nominal enterprise costs. General contractors are becoming procurement specialists and group purchasing organizations (leveraging buying power and spend). Essentially, bid management software is merely a construction-focused procurement tool. The construction management function is becoming mere contract administration and oversight. The subcontractor community continues to move toward design-build business models, and their technical competency and knowledge are increasing. Their BIM and technology expertise is growing and on many projects surpasses that of the entire project team. Technical specialization will continue to advance with subcontractors to drive high-performance production methods for fabrication and installation. New business models are driving subcontractors from design-build to design-build-maintain. This is an effective way to utilize knowledge and assets but also drive annual maintenance revenue without the need to build a new building. Even in an economy in which new construction may be flat, maintenance revenue is stable and, in some cases, is growing due to the need to maintain existing systems versus replacement. There are some general contractors that are providing outsourced building maintenance that involves all aspects of maintenance, including landscape and janitorial. Management of the entire building life cycle means that a contractor has a vested interest in constructing a building that is easily maintainable.

The building product manufacturer has already undergone many changes with streamlining production and supply chain distribution. Many are very sophisticated in their back-office processes. These efficiencies become stifled upon interface with the contractor. This will change as contractors use BIM and create a more efficient interface. BIM will assist in driving more configurable building systems that are semifabricated and delivered to the job site. The continued drive to just-in-time supply chains will minimize on-site fabrication. Use of BIM in design will optimize to prefabrication and less customization. This configuration management will provide a more factory-like approach while providing a custom design that does not appear to be cookie cutter. The experience requirements of installers will continue to be reduced and lower-wage labor that can follow a "color by numbers" approach will become efficient. Because of a configuration-based approach, manufacturer waste will continue to reduce product prices or at least keep the prices stable against any commodity inflationary pressures. The bottom line, less waste is good for everyone, especially the consumer (owner).

The owner is the single most effective "agent of change" in the industry. In order to drive effective change, the owner must become knowledgeable with the mission of being able to ask critical questions without necessarily becoming an expert. Building methods to collect and analyze data drives decision making that is self-evident and defendable. Reliance on a few experts and opinions of those experts is rarely a beneficial system, particularly if those experts do not have aligned interests. In the health care industry, there are companies that provide expense management services. These services are not billed by the hour; rather, fees are based on the rate of success. Essentially, they receive a share of the costs they save a hospital. They have aligned interests with the owner and aligned benefits as well.

Notes

Chapter 1

1. David G. Cotts, Kathy O. Roper, and P. Richard Payant, *The Facility Management Handbook,* 3rd ed. (USA: AMACOM, 2010), 56.
2. Adrian Gostick and Chester Elton, *The Orange Revolution* (USA: Free Press, 2010), 5.

Chapter 2

1. Eliminating Waste in Estimating: Quantity Survey and Payment for Estimating Procedure Recommended to Owners and Investors, Architects, Engineers and Contractors, Approved and Adopted by The American Institute of Architects, The American Engineering Council of the Federated American Engineering Societies, and The Associated General Contractors of America, 1928.

Chapter 3

1. *Encyclopedia Britannica Online,* s.v. "Thomas S. Kuhn," http://www.britannica .com/EBchecked/topic/324460/Thomas-S-Kuhn.
2. Jim Collins, *Good to Great: Why Some Companies Make the Leap . . . and Others Don't* (USA: Harper Business, 2001).

Chapter 4

1. James P. Lewis, *Mastering Project Management: Applying Advanced Concepts of Systems Thinking, Control and Evaluation, and Resource Allocation* (New York: McGraw-Hill, 1998), 111.
2. Barbara Bryson and Canan Yetmen, *The Owner's Dilemma: Driving Success and Innovation in the Design and Construction Industry* (USA: Greenway Communications, 2010).
3. Dictionary.com, http://dictionary.reference.com/browse/enterprise resource planning.
4. Steve Steinhilber, *Strategic Alliances: Three Ways to Make Them Work* (Boston: Harvard Business School Press, 2008), 6–7.
5. Ibid., 6–7.

Chapter 5

1. Irving H. Buchen, "Paradigm Shift Leadership—It's Trickier Than It Appears," *Leadership Excellence* 24, no. 7 (2007): 19–20.
2. Roger Chevalier, "GAP Analysis Revisited," *Performance Improvement* 49, no. 7 (2010): 5–7.
3. Daniel H. Pink, *Drive: The Surprising Truth about What Motivates Us* (USA: Penguin, 2009), 208.
4. Y.-C. Juan and C. Ou-Jang, "Systematic Approach for the Gap Analysis of Business Processes," *International Journal of Production Research* 42, no. 7 (2004): 1325–1364.

5. Buchen, *Paradigm Shift Leadership,* 19–20.
6. Ibid., 19.
7. Norbert Young, Stephen A. Jones, Harvey M. Bernstein, and John E. Gudgel, *BIM Study* (New York: McGraw-Hill, 2009).

Chapter 6

1. Larry Bossidy and Ram Charan, *Execution: The Discipline of Getting Things Done* (USA: Crown, 2002), 7.

Chapter 7

1. Norbert Young, Stephen A. Jones, Harvey M. Bernstein, and John E. Gudgel, *BIM Study* (New York: McGraw-Hill, 2009).

Biographies

K. Pramod Reddy

K. Pramod Reddy is a nationally recognized expert on advanced construction technologies, including building information modeling (BIM). He is a sought-after speaker and industry advisor. K. P. is currently Vice President of BIM Services for ARC, the company that acquired RCMS Group. Before founding RCMS Group, K. P. was Vice President of Operations and Chief Information Officer for Verso Technologies (NASDAQ). While at Verso, he was involved with nearly a dozen mergers and acquisitions of technology companies. Prior to working at Verso, K. P. served as Chief Technology Officer of Cereus Technology Partners, which he founded in 1997, and acted as President and CEO until its acquisition in 1999. During his tenure at both Cereus and Verso, K. P. was deeply involved in technology projects, which included software development and data management.

A second-generation civil engineer, K. P. grew up in the family-owned design–build firm of K. P. Reddy and Associates Pvt. Ltd. (India), which his father started in India after an extensive career in the United States. He began his career as a Project Engineer and Business Development Manager for Law Engineering and Environmental Services (now MACTEC-AMEC).

K. P. is a graduate of the Georgia Institute of Technology and has a Bachelor of Science degree in civil engineering. He is an active alumnus of the Georgia Institute of Technology, serves as a board member for AMPIRIX, is a mentor member for The Indus Entrepreneur (TiE), is an advisory board member for Midtown Bank & Trust, and serves on the board of directors for several privately held companies. K. P. served on the National Council of Architectural Registration Boards (NCARB) BIM Task Force and as an Adjunct Professor at the Georgia Institute of Technology. K. P. lives in Atlanta, Georgia, with his wife Nehal and their two sons.

Arol Wolford, President/CEO SmartBIM

Arol Wolford co-founded SmartBIM, based on his passion for information solutions in the building design and construction industry. Arol has been a well-known entrepreneur in the building products information industry for the past thirty years. He founded Manufacturers' Survey Group in 1975 and five years later entered the construction information industry with the start-up of Construction Market Data (CMD) in Atlanta, Georgia.

As president and CEO of CMD, Arol oversaw the CMD Group of companies, which included such well-known information sources as Association Construction Publications, Architects' First Source, Buildcore Product Source, CanaData, Clark Reports, Construction Market Data (CMD), Cordell Building Information Services, Manufacturers' Survey Associates, and R. S. Means. CMD Group was also part owner of BIMSA/Mexico and Burwood Reports in Southeast Asia. Arol sold CMD Group to Cahners (now Reed Construction Data) in 2000. Arol served on the board of Revit before it was sold to Autodesk and has pursued the goal of empowering architects, engineers, and contractors with Smart BIM objects from building product manufacturers during the last decade.

In 1997, Arol was named honorary member of the American Institute of Architects (AIA) in recognition of his outstanding contribution to the architectural profession. More recently, he was selected to serve on the AIA 150 Committee, the only nonarchitect so honored. Arol holds a degree in biology from Westmont College of California. He is married to Jane, his high school sweetheart, and has two married daughters.

Tony McGaughey

Tony McGaughey is a native of Atlanta, Georgia, and received his undergraduate degree in history from Georgia State University in 1990. Tony has spent the last twelve years working in the AEC industry in various capacities, from managing the daily operations of civil engineering and BIM services firms to managing BIM production teams on three continents. He has also served as the BIM project manager on several large health care and courthouse projects. Through his various positions, Tony has developed an extensive knowledge of the process of BIM implementation and integration.

Abhilasha Jain

Abhilasha Jain is a graduate of the Georgia Institute of Technology with a master's degree in building construction integrated with facility management and holds a bachelor's degree in architecture. She has over five years of experience in the AEC industry in building design and facility management. She has also served as a building information modeling manager and specializes in implementation of BIM for facility management. Apart from being a specialist in BIM management, she is also a facility planner experienced in health care buildings and their facility transitions.

Tripp Whitley

Growing up as an "army brat," Tripp Whitley proudly considers himself an Atlanta native after graduating from Georgia Tech with a Bachelor of Science degree in civil engineering. During his tenure, he was named "Mr. Georgia Tech," and remains actively involved on campus as an alumnus and donor. Tripp has worked as a civil engineer with both Kimley-Horn and Jordan Engineering, eventually moving to the Autodesk channel as a sales engineer, where he consulted and trained AEC clients in both Civil 3D and Revit implementation. Joining K.P.'s efforts in 2005, Tripp has helped hundreds of clients successfully migrate through the "paradigm shift" that BIM is shaping within our industry. As a BIM expert, he is currently advising Disney, FedEx, Safeway, and other Fortune 500 companies on technology implementation.

Index

American Council of the Federated
American Engineering Societies, 56
American Institute of Architects, 56
Analytics, 63, 183–215
champion assignment, 201–202
findings and conclusions, 213–214
key performance indicators, 193–198
owner research, 196, 199–201
research methods, 202–207
return-on-investment model, 189–193
summary of information, 207–212
ArchiCAD, 45, 143
Architect's BIM, 43–48, 65
As-built records, 34, 36
Asset management, 11–12, 14
Associated General Contractors of
America, 56
Authors, users vs., 199–200
Authoritative approval, 24
Authority, 200
AutoCAD, 118, 135, 143
Autodesk, 143, 156

Benchmarking, 75, 189–193
Bentley BIM (Microstation), 143, 144, 156
Bill of materials, 25
BIM coordinators, 121–122
BIM library, 60
content and specification library,
173–176
for government projects, 67
SMARTBIM Library, 52, 61
BIM library managers, 60, 61
BIM mission statement, 208
BIM objects, 51
for collaboration, 59–61
for different design stages, 63
preapproved, 79
in quantity surveys, 55
in submittal process, 58–59
BIM objectives, 208–209
BIM owner's representative, 175–176
BIM requirements document, 79–114,
167–170

deliverables in, 87–91
execution in, 91–114
general requirements in, 81–86
BIM vision statement, 208
Boiling the ocean approach, 146, 178–179
Buchen, Irving, 163
Building information modeling (BIM),
1–39, 217–220
and construction process/costs, 28–31
cost of software, 120
database sets for, 6
defining, 1
and design guidelines, 26–28
different purposes of, 41
for enhanced communication, 23–24
for facility management, 10–16
future trends in, 6–10
for government organizations, 41–42
history of, 3–6
legal/liability issues with, 42
main objectives for, 41
owners' incentives to implement, 17–20
and preventive maintenance, 35–37
in procurement, 24–26
standards for, 42, 43
for sustainability, 31–35
user experience with, 20–23
Building life cycle, 68, 70
Building management systems, 8–10
Building product manufacturers (BPMs),
8, 50, 54, 219
Building product manufacturer's BIM,
50–65
building product submittals, 58–59
green analysis and simulation, 62–65
product catalogs, 59–62
quantity surveys, 52–58
Building product submittals, 58–59
Build intent model, 6
Business rules, 211

California Code of Regulations, 32
Catalogs, product, 59–62
Cell phones, 126, 133, 134